HOLY GROUND
The Guide to Faith and Ecology

Sponsored and Supported by

The Alliance of Religions and Conservation

World Wide Fund for Nature

MOA International

THE SACRED LAND
PROJECT

The Sacred Land Project

Holy Ground

The Guide to Faith and Ecology

Edited by
JO EDWARDS
and
MARTIN PALMER

PILKINGTON PRESS

FIRST PUBLISHED 1997
BY PILKINGTON PRESS LTD
YELVERTOFT MANOR
NORTHAMPTONSHIRE NN6 6LF

ISBN 1 899044 12 4

PRODUCED, DESIGNED AND TYPESET BY:
A.H. JOLLY (EDITORIAL) LTD
YELVERTOFT MANOR
NORTHAMPTONSHIRE NN6 6LF

PRINTED IN GREAT BRITAIN

CONTENTS

From WELCOMES
after the Venerable Kushok Bakula

Your bowed, bared shaven head –
Deep-set cheeks and sunken, all-seeing eyes…
At the very moment you thought you were free to retire –
You had to take on the whole burden of your world
Like a cross, there, on your shoulders:

Bodhisattva.

How many of you are willing to lose your names?

    Then yours will be the Shining Throne

      – the true place of light where you are seated, within.

Jay Ramsay

Note
Jay Ramsay's poems are taken from *The Windsor Sequence* written after the Summit on Religions and Conservation at Windsor Castle in May 1995, where he was poet in residence, with artist Xavier Pick.

PREFACE

WHAT DO the great faiths of the world have to say about the environmental crisis? And even more importantly, what are they doing about the current state of the environment?

For over a decade now, the World Wide Fund for Nature International (WWF) has been asking the faiths precisely those questions. They have done so, not in any sense of superiority but in genuine interest in the potential within and amongst the faiths to create a deeper and more sustainable commitment to good environmental practice.

This whole adventure began in 1986 when WWF invited five of the world's major religions – Buddhism, Christianity, Hinduism, Islam and Judaism – to come to Assisi in Italy, birthplace of the Christian saint of ecology, St. Francis and to share what each faith had to say about nature. Here the five faiths made a commitment to act on their teachings and to make ecology, conservation and the environment a focus of their actions and their prayers.

Over the next few years, four other faiths joined, each making a written commitment and beginning action programmes. They were; the Bahá'ís in 1987; the Sikhs in 1989; the Jains in 1991 and the Taoists in 1995.

By 1995 over 120,000 religiously based environmental projects were up and running world wide, often assisted by WWF but many springing directly from religious convictions and commitment, awoken as if from a long slumber. By 1995, the United Nations could comment that the programme of working with major religions had reached 'untold millions' with the conservation message. Millions whom no other source could have reached.

This was why, in 1995, in Japan and then at Windsor Castle, England, leaders from the nine religions and conservationists, leaders from the worlds of media, banking and other interested bodies, attended the Summit on Religions and Conservation. From this came a renewed commitment to work on ecological programmes. From it came the new international structure designed to facilitate this – the Alliance of Religions and Conservation – ARC. From this also came the poems and the sketches which so enliven this book, product of the Summit poet, Jay Ramsay and the Summit artist, Xavier Pick.

At Windsor, the faiths looked back over the growth of their involvement and looked forward to its expansion. They looked at ways to reach yet more faithful with the message of care for nature and of ways in which they could collaborate with each other and with secular bodies.

This is the strength of the programme of religions and conservation groups working together. This is what this book celebrates and we hope encourages further.

The book has three main sections.

PART 1 contains insights from the three groups who now carry the responsibility of organising assistance to the world religions by the conservation world through ARC (the Alliance of Religions and Conservation).

PART 2 contains the fundamental teachings of the nine faiths, drawing upon the documents produced for Assisi or just after as well as the revised foundation documents of each faith, produced for the Japan and Windsor Summits.

PART 3 looks at practical outcomes ranging from the important inter-faith initiative on the use of religiously owned land – the Ohito Declaration – to actual projects on the ground.

PART ONE

Reflections on Religion and Conservation

THE JOURNEYS OF THE FAITHS
From Assisi To Windsor
Theory and Practice

HIS ROYAL HIGHNESS THE PRINCE PHILIP, DUKE of EDINBURGH, was until 1996, International President of the World Wide Fund for Nature International. As such, it was at his suggestion that the Assisi meeting of 1986 was held, bringing together the five main faiths for the first time with leading conservation groups. Since then, his unstinting support and encouragement of the programme to link religions to conservation has enabled much to take place and his visits to many of the projects has focused media attention on this unexpected alliance between the secular and religious worlds.

In his paper, Prince Philip looks at the growth of the alliance from Assisi to Windsor and reflects upon its significance.

President Kawai heads a major Japanese humanitarian group, MOA, linked with Shintoism, the ancient religion of Japan. The support of MOA and in particular of President Kawai, enabled the Summit to take place. Early on in the progress towards the Summit, his son, Terumichi Kawai played a key role. His untimely and tragic death in 1994 brought sadness to us all. But the spirit of what he sought to do, lives on in this paper by President Kawai.

Brian Pilkington of the Pilkington Foundation, chairs the Alliance of Religions and Conservation and guides the development of projects and work with the faiths in the aftermath of the Summit. In his paper he looks at what has already started to happen and at how ARC relates to both the religious and environmental worlds.

Poems by Jay Ramsay, court poet to the Summit, and pictures by Xavier Pick, court artist, offer their understanding and experiences of the Windsor Summit, drawing upon music, dance, liturgy and prayers from the nine religions to explore our relationship with the physical world.

Ivan Hattingh's paper reflects both his scientific background and his passion for the environment. The whole involvement of religion with ecology springs from a project his department at WWF UK initiated on religion and ecology through a school text book project. From 1983 onwards Ivan has supported and encouraged the expansion of this work world wide. Here he reflects upon the nature of the environmental threats facing the planet.

Martin Palmer has run WWF's programme on work with religions since 1983. He devised the Assisi event and has led the major initiatives on religion and ecology world wide. He organised the Summit and now acts as secretary general to ARC. From his wide experience of religion in action he comments forcefully on what religion brings to conservation and what problems religion highlights in contemporary environmental work.

THE ROAD FROM ASSISI TO WINDSOR
HRH The Prince Philip
Duke of Edinburgh

A T ASSISI IN 1986, a seed was planted by the leaders of five of the great religious communities of the world with WWF acting as the technical adviser. We all hoped that it would germinate and take root. For my part, I would have been satisfied if the seed had reproduced a healthy and vigorous shrub, but it has done far better than even the most optimistic could have hoped. It has grown into a sturdy tree, whose branches are providing a refuge for birds and insects, whose leaves are providing shade for the animals and plants which live on the earth, and whose roots play an important part in the survival of all those that live under the earth. It also represents every plant in the waters and seas on which all aquatic life depends.

The seed was the Network on Religion and Conservation, but it has since undergone a metamorphosis and is now flourishing as the Alliance of Religions and Conservation, thanks to the generous support and nourishment it has received from its three sponsors; WWF, MOA and the Pilkington Foundation.

Like a tree, the Alliance has grown almost imperceptibly as it put down its roots and added new branches. The full extent of that growth was revealed during the highly successful preparatory meeting for this Summit, recently concluded in Japan. I am much encouraged by the nature and extent of the projects undertaken by the members of the Alliance to promote the conservation of nature.

While it is useful and encouraging for those directly involved in the conservation of nature to know about the achievements of the members of the Alliance, the measure of success is not the publicity it generates, but the practical impact and effect of those achievements on the health and vitality of the natural environment.

Make no mistake, the health of our planet and the number and diversity of its living species are under very serious threat. The natural systems of the atmosphere around the planet, and its rivers, lakes and oceans are being polluted by human and toxic effluents to an alarming extent. Species are being exploited or having their habitat destroyed and are becoming extinct at a faster rate than has ever been recorded. Our planet Earth should be seen as a giant organism and its health depends on the combined effect of all these factors.

This globe of ours has been spinning in space for a very long time and it has been subjected to some fairly rough treatment. Temperatures have fallen to create ice-ages and risen to encourage dense vegetation. The moving of tectonic plates has changed the shapes of land and sea masses and it has been battered by meteorites from space. All these are natural phenomena, but the present situation is not due to any of these.

The only significant factor that coincides with the deterioration of the planet's health over the last century is the dramatic increase in the world's human population, which began some two hundred years ago. The key issue for the conservation of our natural environment is to find ways of protecting it from the consequences of the human explosion.

If these consequences are to be controlled and modified, certain vital actions will need to be taken.

It is absolutely vital to ensure that its natural resources, on which all life on earth depends, are not exploited faster than they can regenerate. This applies particularly to endangered species of plants and animals and to the fish of the oceans and the few remaining natural forests. This means that the areas of the world which contain the richest diversity of species must be given effective protection from human encroachment and disturbance. It also means much stricter control of poaching and the illegal trade in endangered species through more effective support for the convention on International Trade in Endangered Species. If this is not done, there is a serious risk that the present high rate at which species are becoming extinct will reach dangerous proportions.

It is absolutely vital to ensure that there is sufficient forest cover to absorb the ever-increasing quantity of carbon dioxide being dumped into the atmosphere by human activities. If this is not done, the warming of the global climate will put both human communities and important natural eco-systems at risk.

It is absolutely vital to ensure that noxious gases are not allowed to escape into the atmosphere to cause changes to its functions that could adversely affect all life on earth.

It is absolutely vital to ensure that the vegetation cover of less fertile soils is maintained so that the soil is not eroded to cause siltation in rivers, mangrove swamps and coral reefs. Much fertile land has already been lost and it would be folly to needlessly reduce the capacity of the oceans to provide food for human consumption.

It is absolutely vital to ensure that waste material of all sorts – nuclear, industrial, household rubbish and human effluents – are made safe and innocuous before being released into the natural environment.

It is absolutely vital to ensure that the processes of extracting the earth's mineral deposits do not cause pollution through faulty techniques or leakage; that all damage is repaired and that there is no danger of future damage when the resource has been exhausted.

None of these things can be achieved unless the people who make the decisions understand their necessity, even when it entails extra costs, and unless ordinary people appreciate their general responsibility for the future health of the planet.

The members of both urban as well as rural communities need to understand the relationship between the physical systems that sustain life on this planet – the atmosphere and weather systems; the ocean currents; the water cycles between the oceans, the clouds and the rainfall; the carbon cycle and the natural drainage and irrigation functions of the river systems.

These are all the facts of life of our planet; it is only the response to them that raises moral issues. There is the purely practical response that life on earth is immensely diverse and that this diversity has great scientific interest, and should therefore be protected. There is the aesthetic response that the world and everything in it is beautiful and wonderful and that it is for this reason that we should care for it. Then there is the moral response that suggests that the present generation has a moral obligation to pass on an undamaged natural heritage to future generations. There is also the religious response, which is based on the belief that the universe, and particularly this planet, is the creation, or was the inspiration of, a supreme being and that therefore all believers have a religious duty to avoid doing any damage to it.

All these responses demand a degree of altruism on the part of the human population. There is, of course, one other possible response and that is the purely selfish view that only human requirements need to be taken into consideration. In other words, that all we need to worry about is the human environment.

Whatever the motive, the fact is that if this generation is to leave the earth in a fit state for our successors, we will need to address the consequences of human activities and address them urgently.

I am quite sure that each religious community has its own reasons for being concerned about the state of our planet. It is not for me to suggest how, or by what means the religious communities should respond to this concern, but I would like to propose certain basic principles:

1   The extinction of a single species of wild plant or animal life is far more significant than the death of a number of individuals of a domestic or even of a wild species that is not threatened with extinction. I believe it is also important to make a distinction between direct threats to the survival of species, and attitudes to the treatment of animals. The former is a matter of fact, the latter is a matter of personal perception.

2   Much attention is being paid to what are known as animal rights. It goes

without saying that all animals should be treated with consideration, but we have to face three distinct problems, (i) the exploitation of wild species for human consumption, either as food or for their products; (ii) the treatment and slaughter of domestic animals; and (iii) the treatment of what are considered to be vermin and pests or the cause of human diseases.

3   All living species depend for their survival on making use of some other species. Some depend on plants, others depend on other animals, yet others survive on re-cycling dead matter. That is the way the natural system works, however much some people may regret it. The essential criterion is that no species should be allowed to put another at risk of extinction.

4   The sheer size of the human population on this planet means that humanity today has a far more significant influence on the natural environment than ever before. Nature is no longer able to be self-regulating. Humanity has interfered to the extent of making species extinct; it must now interfere to help nature to regulate blatant imbalances in the system, which humanity itself created. In order to give some threatened species a chance of survival, it may be necessary to control the numbers and distribution of their more successful competitors or predators.

5   It is possible to convince some people by facts and rational argument that the earth is facing serious problems, and these people may then act appropriately. Others simply cannot comprehend that sort of argument. They need to see the issue in a more romantic light and to have their emotions stirred. Such people are only likely to take appropriate action if they come to believe that they are under a moral obligation to act. It is these people who are most likely to respond to the teaching of their religion. However, I would like to enter one note of caution. Strong emotional feelings or intuition are not alternatives to knowledge. It is the combination of knowledge and comprehension that is the basis of wise decisions.

6   Religions can influence the situation in three ways; (i) they can teach the young about the facts of the natural world and about the natural systems upon which all life depends; (ii) they can take direct action by active leadership in the initiation of practical conservation projects, and (iii) they can preach to, and seek to persuade their members that each individual has a moral obligation to contribute in some way to the conservation of the world's natural systems, and they can suggest how this can best be done. Needless to say, the leadership must know what it is doing and talking about if it is to have any significant beneficial effect.

The members of the Alliance have already demonstrated that they can make very important contributions to the resolution of this crisis and I have every confidence that they will re-double their efforts and that they will come to have a decisive influence on human thoughts and actions.

I cannot emphasise too strongly that the world is in a critical state and, whatever it may look like from the comfort of an apparently secure urban per-spective, time for the natural environment is running out, and it is running out fast. If you are in the process of blowing up a balloon there is nothing to warn you that it is about to burst. We are stretching the earth's systems like a small child blowing up a balloon. If it goes on blowing, the crucial question is 'when is it going to burst?'

THE HEALING OF THE EARTH

Teruaki Kawai

President, MOA International

J
T IS MOA's great privilege to be a co-sponsor of this historic Summit, to-
gether with the World Wide Fund for Nature International, and the
Pilkington Foundation.

As everyone knows, in Japan we have the Shinto faith. Shinto has arisen
within Japanese culture as an indigenous religion. Unlike many other major
religions, Shinto has neither a founder, nor a defined set of beliefs. Shinto has
in fact grown out of our awareness and appreciation of nature.

Japanese people believe that life pervades everything on earth, including
mountains, rivers, animals, plants and human beings. Within this life, they perceive the Divine. In this manner, Japanese people believe in the existence of
many kinds of gods and deities. Moreover, the Japanese believe that living
beings live out their lives within the grand scheme established by the gods.
They believe that when a person dies, the spirit continues to live on eternally,
although the body returns to the earth.

Many other religions have flourished in Japan, co-existing with Shinto and
influencing it.

In particular, Buddhism and Shinto have been the two major religious
influences on the Japanese people. Japanese Buddhism has dropped most of the
specific precepts that it inherited from India and has reinforced traditional Japanese attitudes which inform reverence for nature. Buddhism clearly expresses
respect for nature, as this scripture shows; 'Plants and earth can become Bud-
dhas, because all beings, sentient and non-sentient, have the Buddha-nature'.

Thus, everything on earth – grass, stones, everything – has life. Life is con-
nected with the Absolute. This Buddhist idea formed the essence of traditional
Japanese aesthetics, permeating all aspects of Japanese art.

The idea that the whole universe is a living thing is not only common to
both Buddhism and Shinto, but is an idea that is fundamental to early civilisation.
It is now becoming popular to respect these traditional beliefs and to adopt
them into our modern society. This opinion implies the following concerns and
raises many questions: whether or not the environment is merely the physical

things that surround us; whether or not we think humanity is the centre of the universe; and is it enough just to repair and maintain the physical aspect of the environment which humanity destroyed; furthermore, does environmental conservation require us to adopt spiritual values instead of material values?

If we ask whether these considerations are commonplace amongst ordinary people, and amongst existing conservationists, we must answer, 'No'.

In this sense it is clear that the role of religious leaders in combating environmental destruction is crucial.

There are of course many approaches to environmental conservation and it is impossible and unnecessary for religious leaders to take on all of them. But it is indispensable for religions and religious leaders to identify a set of values which is needed as a foundation for our civilization of tomorrow. Re-evaluation of spiritual values is the most important agenda for humanity. Situations of the modern day tend to make many leaders concerned with the well-being of one nation or one race, and adopt a 'symptom treatment' approach in coping with difficult problems. Therefore, the role of religion in the global perspective is extremely important.

A teaching of one faith says that since God granted various talents and abilities to man, man is obliged to use these talents in a righteous way to protect God's creation as a steward of the Earth.

A teaching of one faith says that since God created man as a micro-cosmos man is capable of fulfilling his mission in accordance with the will of the Universe.

A teaching of one faith says that since God created man as a being closest to God, man should protect all life in nature because it belongs to God.

A teaching of one faith says everything in the Universe is related to each other and no single entity exists by itself. Therefore, man must maintain reverence for nature not only for the sake of others, but also his own sake, as part of the web of life.

The Assisi Conference was epoch-making for two reasons: firstly, it acknowledged the essence of each faith's teachings on the dignity of nature and secondly, it affirmed the proper direction for our civilization.

Since the Event was held, a range of activities based on these teachings have been carried out.

I have been asked to address the issue of 'The Healing of the Earth'.

Actually this is much too big an issue for me to tackle on my own, but I nonetheless wish to share my convictions with you. I believe that it is vital to act and expand upon the spirit of the Assisi Event, based as it was on the leadership and wisdom of HRH Prince Philip. To harness this spirit in specific plans means to enable the lives and roles of all living things – mountains, rivers, trees and grasses, birds, animals, fish, even insects – to be fulfilled to their greatest extent. This will then lead to 'the healing of the earth'.

At the same time, when I ask myself how we can put the spirit of the Assisi Event into practice, I realise that we are facing many challenges. Mokichi Okada, whom we at MOA love and respect most, stated simply that the Earth is a living entity and that humanity is a part of that entity. What he meant by this is that the earth is composed of invisible spirit and physical substance, which together create an energy that forms the basis of all life. Based on this philosophy, in 1936 Okada began to advocate an agricultural method, later referred to as Nature Farming, that allowed the natural power inherent in the soil to produce the most nutritious plants.

In the same year, Okada originated the medical art of the technique of Jorei. This is a method of concentrating the natural energy of the fire, water, and earth elements, which pervades the universe, and efficaciously directing it at the human body in order to heal.

As I mentioned at the beginning, the Japanese view of nature is based on the co-existence of humanity with nature recognising the existence of the Divine within everything in the natural world. Okada found strict law governing the natural world. That is nature's mechanism: that through rain, wind, light and heat from the sun, the impurities accumulated on the Earth may be purified. Okada developed his principle of purification based on this understanding of nature and further applied it to contemporary society.

He taught that disease itself is a part of the process of purification. This process begins when the clouds produced in the spirit due to the repetition of thoughts, speech, and deeds that run counter to nature, reach a certain level. In other words, he viewed our disease as being a gift from nature, which purifies us.

The medical art of Jorei is a means of reinforcing this natural purification process in our daily lives to eliminate invisible spiritual clouds, even when we are enjoying good health. Jorei is also applicable when we are ill.

Okada also taught that the beauty of nature, and of great works of art, also has the power to purify our bodies and spirits. Based on this idea, Okada initiated a wide range of cultural activities, collected superb works of art, and constructed art museums to make all of these available to a wide audience.

The idea that underpinned all of Okada's activities was that the essence of life is the fusion of spirit and body. The word 'healing' is derived from the Greek word, *holos*, meaning whole, which is also the origin of the word 'health'. This fact points to the importance of seeing the whole system of living beings, including the environment and humanity, as interconnected. If we fail to do this, it will be impossible to realise the healing of the earth and humanity.

Although I am not qualified to speak about this in detail, I am aware that each religious faith has a valuable tradition of healing and teachings concerning the integrity of nature.

Based on the spirit of the Assisi Event, we should all make efforts to put such teachings into practice and to generate tangible results that will be obvious to all. In this manner, we will be able to develop alongside and with secular society a mode of living that is based on an awareness of the true relation between humanity and our environment. This will indeed be a great turning-point for the modern world, overly based as it is on material and economic values.

If we are able to achieve a dialogue with secular conservation groups, rather than assume a critical or antagonistic relationship, a harmonious and effective environmental movement will be developed, and we can advance together.

However, it is necessary to point out that there will be many difficulties on the way. Taking the example of MOA Nature Farming, we realised that it was important that its theory and practice not be presented in the context of a religious activity, in order to avoid it being seen as self-righteous. I also believe it is important that Jorei should establish its value objectively, and not be seen as some kind of faith-healing or ritualistic exercise.

Medical science is continuously advancing. Notably, medical equipment is now very sophisticated. But, it is a reality that the safety of human life is still threatened by incurable diseases. The quality of the morality and ethics of medicine has been questioned. In my opinion, it is no longer appropriate to think that only the physicians can deal with improving the conditions of human life. Rather, people of all different disciplines who are concerned with the betterment of human health must participate in safe-guarding human lives. In this sense, the value of traditional healing practices of different faiths must be re-evaluated and revived in this modern world in such a way that the general public can accept and incorporate into their healthcare practices. I believe that the underlying teachings and philosophy of each faith's traditional healing practices can no doubt lead us towards healing the planet Earth. I am hoping that our practice of Jorei will be supported by scientific evidence from doctors and medical institutions in the field of comprehensive medicine, which is now progressing remarkably, so that people in society today will be able to acknowledge its value.

We at MOA believe that art and cultural activities should not be confined to some elite set of people, but instead we are trying to create a world in which the beauty of nature and of the arts is present in our daily lives.

It is also important, just as Mokichi Okada said, that we use simple and clear language to explain our beliefs, so that it is not only those of an intellectual bent and believers who can understand our philosophy but ordinary people as well. In this way, we can actually put our ideas and beliefs into practice and joyfully share the benevolence of nature.

Another conviction that I would like to share with you concerns the importance of building up trusting relationships between like-minded individuals and organisations, so that together we can pursue our common goals. I became especially aware of this during discussions at the Conference on Religions, the Land and Conservation, and at the first Session of this Summit. Indeed, the very way in which WWF, the Pilkington Foundation, and MOA have worked together with the major religions for the Summit is a model. Just as His Royal Highness Prince Philip mentioned, strong bonds among different faiths were created in the first session in Japan by their concerted efforts to protect the Earth which is in a critical state. Respecting each others' teachings and traditions, I believe the faiths must act on the basis of mutual trust and co-operation.

I am convinced that the newly-born Alliance of Religions and Conservation will vigorously help to realise the wishes of each faith in their efforts for environmental protection.

I am delighted to announce MOA's official support for ARC.

In conclusion, I would like to offer a prayer that dialogue between the delegates of the various faiths represented here at Windsor Castle, and between religious and secular society, will make it possible for us to act and expand upon the Assisi spirit and that together we may begin to heal the Earth actively and swiftly. With that sincere wish and prayer, I would like to conclude my greetings.

MAKING THE ALLIANCE OF RELIGIONS AND CONSERVATION A REALITY

BRIAN PILKINGTON
Chairman of the Trustees

THE PHILOSOPHY of the Alliance of Religions and Conservation was evolved at the Windsor Summit drawing upon the activities of the WWF which had been collaborating with the religions on projects conserving wildlife and habitats. Since the conference ARC has developed in a way that reflects the growing interest globally of the major religions in the protection of the environment and particularly the use of the sacred lands in their possession. It has been fascinating to observe the momentum with which new ideas and projects have been undertaken and to find that a positive response has been accorded to conservation throughout the world by spiritual leaders and their followers at a time when concern for the future of the global environment has never been at a higher level. The most rewarding aspect of this development is the ease with which secular advisors and even non-religious governmental organisations have collaborated with the religious sector for the agreed goals of environmental protection. The continuing success of ARC is due to this new 'spirit of the age' at once both practical and idealistic. Let me provide some examples.

The new interplay between the secular and the religious is amply demonstrated by the 'leveraging' power of ARC to encourage funding from religious bodies when ARC endorses a new and exciting environmental project. Our project at Tel Ada in Syria is a good example. The Tel Ada Centre is a unique Christian/Muslim venture to rebuild the oldest monastery in Syria of the Syrian Orthodox Church as an interfaith and environmental studies centre. The monastic lands will be developed to illustrate to neighbouring farmers, how organic farming can work. The monastery will become a major centre for organic farming and for environmental teaching aimed at Muslims and Christians alike. Through ARC's involvement, other bodies such as the Vatican and Orthodox communities in the USA, have begun to offer funds – as the project is seen to be taken seriously by an outside group such as ARC. Likewise in China in one of the most outstanding projects yet undertaken we have gained both financial and staffing support from the China Taoist Association and the Religious Affairs Bureau. ARC is funding a detailed survey of Taoist sacred mountains which have retained a purity and integrity which is missing from many other mountain sites in China. In recent years these have come under threat mainly from tourism – both religious pilgrimage and general tourism. The Taoists, working in collaboration with the Chinese Tourist Board, can now jointly plan an appropriate future for some of the most beautiful sacred mountain sites in the world. ARC is particularly proud of this achievement in one of the fastest growing and most environmentally threatened countries in the world where we have helped forge links between religion, the State and the environmental groups in a way never previously undertaken. In India we have worked effectively with the Hindu community supporting the conservation of lands in Vrindavan – the sacred forest of Krishna. This project began with tree-planting as a focus, but has since extended to embrace a much wider range of environmental activities. In particular ARC has funded educational outreach designed to assist pilgrims and citizens of Vrindavan to understand and participate more fully in this project and to bring this activity to the attention of Hindu communities world-wide, enabling them to appreciate the significance of this initiative undertaken by the local community and its friends.

ARC thus emerges as a helpful catalyst bringing together communities and focusing an international spotlight on worthwhile projects which would otherwise have gone unnoticed and underfunded.

Projects can be assisted in various ways dependent on the specific nature of what is being undertaken. Let me illustrate how ARC has participated in helping our associates around the world. One of the main requirements of anyone working in the field of conservation is of course education. It is vital that texts and teaching can reach those places where young audiences are eager to learn but where educational resources are stretched. In Zambia, for example, we have funded an interfaith educational project in schools. This is to assist in the production of the Conservation Unit of a new Religious Education course for senior secondary school pupils. Other projects require physical participation in the working of the land and I would like to quote the exciting project in Russia where sacred land fallen into disuse and neglect has been reactivated with a view to long term and environmentally efficient land use. The lands of the Spasso-Preobrazhensky Monastery, in Valaam, Russia suffered severe pollution and neglect during the Soviet occupation of the island when the monastery became a military training centre. ARC funding has assisted a practical project involved in the restoration of the gardens and orchards on the monastic lands. In projects such as this, ARC's unique ability to call upon WWF's international conservation expertise and ICOREC's unparalleled expertise in the field of religion, means we can properly assess and then assist such major schemes. Respect for the value systems of communities in any part of the world is central to the philosophy of ARC. We try to ensure that projects are based on sound research and a full understanding of the ecology of a region. Here ARC can again provide the necessary expertise to analyse environments and provide models for planning and development. In, for example, China, Russia and India we have assisted in this fashion and helped to plan for the future and to encourage deeper involvement in the understanding of the impact of tourism on ecology – one of the critical problems emerging in the latter part of the twentieth century with the vast growth in global travel. This is particularly relevant where ARC is working on major pilgrimage sites such as Jain or Taoist holy mountains, or historic sites such as the Shrine of the Virgin Mary at Walsingham in the UK.

Sometimes religious groups hold land that is of especial significance, often sites of outstanding natural beauty. On such sites ongoing projects can provide models of environmental conservation and ARC is particularly anxious to promote work which can be visited and provide exemplars for other communities around the world. Vrindavan in India, is one such site. Another is Mount Athos in northern Greece. This unique monastic run peninsula is one of the most important natural environments left in the Mediterranean and ARC has funded a major work camp of Orthodox youth leaders on Mount Athos, which assist the Church/WWF Greece projects on the Holy Mountain and helps train future leaders in the Orthodox world, especially Eastern Europe.

A special ARC project is the promotional work in relation to the Ohito Declaration on Religion, Land and Conservation. This declaration was put together at an interfaith conference held in Japan in April 1995 and presented to the Summit of Religions and Conservation. Its focus is the environmental use of religious farming land and the principles which should guide this. Steps are now being taken to systematically promote the Declaration world-wide and get across its main message, which is education at all levels, with a particular emphasis on promoting education in this area through practical land based projects. In its first year, the Declaration was presented to three separate workshops, two in Europe and the third in Africa. We are particularly grateful to our colleagues in MOA for their support of this project.

Here then are some examples of the ways in which ARC has been operating world-wide to develop its work amongst the world's great religions and the conservation movement. What will the future hold? We will of course continue the work that we have been doing and try to develop awareness as to how the environmental problems of this age can best be addressed through religion and conservation. We hope to continue to encourage religions to maintain the interest that they have now been manifesting and to strengthen their levels of input into conservation problems. Perhaps most of all we would like to let the whole world know that the religions are no longer dormant in their concern for the future of the world's environment and that together with the conservation movement a huge new force can be unleashed world-wide for the benefit of the global environment and all the beings that depend for their survival on its well-being.

CLOSING THE LOOP
Ivan Hattingh
WWF UK

I WAS FIRST INVOLVED in working with faith groups when we in WWF published, back in 1984, a book looking at the creation stories of eight different faith groups, and how these stories affected the way they related to Nature. It immediately became a best seller and was translated into many languages. As a result we were asked by His Royal Highness Prince Philip to organise the first gathering of the Faiths to consider their response to the environmental problems faced by the earth. The result was the Assisi Meeting, which this meeting celebrates.

I speak as a trained scientist, who has seen the error of his ways and wishes to make amends to you, as the keepers of vast knowledge and rich traditions.

There is no doubt that humans are inventive and ingenious. When faced with alarming problems, it seems this ingenuity usually finds solutions. The history of the world is a history of inventions.

And the tools we can use with this ingenuity become more and more astonishing. The technology push which is occurring at the moment, and which comes largely from Japan, means that by the turn of the century computers will have one thousand times the power of today's machines and the development time for them will be one tenth of the development time in 1995.

It is this ingenuity which enables us to provide housing, warmth, energy, food and education for numbers of people and at a level which futurologists of twenty five years ago (Did futurologists exist 25 years ago?) predicted would lead to a complete breakdown of human societies in many parts of the world. Yes, human ability to resolve complex problems is truly remarkable and must be recognised.

Yet paging through the Worldwatch Institute's State of the World Report for 1995, which is subtitled – a report on progress toward a sustainable society – one can be forgiven a despairing sigh.

It does not seem that progress is the most appropriate word to describe the trends in environmental change, which show little deviation from the previous years' trends. There certainly has been progress of a sort in some parts of the world but this progress can only be measured in bags of product or bags of waste. The real problem is that we still accept quantity as a measure of progress. A linear progression… seed plus soil plus necessary chemicals plus water plus light equals good harvest… is how we see it.

Information technology and particularly the super highway (the means by which vast quantities of information can be transmitted to vast numbers of people in the blink of an eye) are held up as a way in which we can overcome our most intractable problems. But the very language 'Super Highway' suggests linearity, getting from point A to point B, which has nothing to do with the way nature works. We have plenty of knowledge, but what seems to be lacking is wisdom.

And wisdom, I would contend comes from social pull. Computers cannot be plonked in to a situation to change matters. They won't. Information Technology does not favour one thing or another, centralisation or decentralisation, it makes both possible. The important decisions that have to be made are social decisions. And it is lack of society's influence on decision making (which has increasingly passed to narrowly focused specialists) that I feel we should be looking at.

I should like to start by examining in closer detail just three areas of nature on which the 'State of the World Report 1995' comments. These are the fish resources of the earth, the water supplies and finally the soil on which humans grow crops to feed themselves.

Human numbers

In September 1994 the delegates of 179 countries met in Cairo at the Conference on Population and Development. One of the points which was discussed at the conference was; How many people can the earth support? and what will limit the numbers of these people? Will it be scarcity of food, scarcity of water, damaging levels of pollution or some other controlling factor?

It seems clear to me that all of these factors and many more will exert a controlling influence on human populations but shortage of food will have the first influence. The oceans and more precisely the harvesting of the oceans has already exceeded the levels which could be considered sustainable.

The future of fish

Twenty years ago, a marine biologist working for the Food and Agriculture Organisation of the United Nations estimated that 100 million tons was the maximum yield that ocean fisheries could sustain without damaging their future. This figure was reached in 1989. (And incidentally that was exactly the same amount as the world production of beef and poultry combined in the same year.) During the following four years the total catch fluctuated between 97 million and 99 million tons despite improved harvesting methods. This of course means that after taking increase of population into account the fish catch per person dropped by 8% in four years.

Recent reports suggest that all of the world's 17 major fishing areas are now either being harvested at their maximum capacity or beyond it. This means that at the most optimistic, the future of fish in the diet of the average person will decline steadily until the population stabilises or fish farming provides substantially more than it is providing at present.

Pollution and over-harvesting are together denuding many coastal estuaries and inland seas. The Aral Sea, which used to yield up to 44,000 tons of fish a year has now shrunk, and as a result of the diversion of rivers for agricultural use, has become so saline that all of the 24 species of fish that were once harvested for food are now apparently extinct.

Oysters have been gathered in the Chesapeake Bay in the United States for many years and 100 years ago 100,000 tons of oyster flesh, not including the shells, were harvested annually. Now, as a result of over-harvesting, serious pollution and disease, less than 1000 tons were harvested in 1993.

And the economic effects of the destruction of fisheries is striking. What used to be a cheap source of protein for people who could not afford meat has now become more expensive than beef.

In some cases, prices of fish have reached astronomical heights. For example a 300 kg bluefin tuna caught in the North Atlantic was sold to an agent for exclusive sushi restaurants in Tokyo for $80,000.

Water, a wasted asset
The damming and diversion of river water onto the land to enable more crops to be produced is one of the earliest achievements of humans. It is not surprising then to discover that a breakdown in the irrigation systems led to the decline of these same civilisations.

During the several millennia during which irrigation was practised it spread all over the world and since 1950 the growth in irrigated lands became particularly rapid with 150 million hectares being added.

This was largely achieved by diverting and damming river waters but also by using the underground water tables by drilling wells. And the important thing to be recognised about drawing water from water tables is that the rate at which the water is used must not exceed the rate at which the water is replenished… and this can be measured very accurately.

Irrigation systems are expensive and this was a major focus of capital expenditure by the development agencies and National governments. But the benefits of intensive cropping enables great increases in food production. Where temperatures permit year round cropping, two or even three crops per year can be produced where previously a meagre single crop was obtained.

Since the early '60s, the use of underground water by drilling wells for irrigation has been greatly increased and when used at the village level, this almost always produces beneficial results for the villagers. But ingenious humans do not seem to be able to get too much of a good thing. In many of the more arid parts of the world, when one flies in an aircraft, one is aware of vast bright green circles where rotating irrigation systems use ground water to produce crops in areas where previously little food grew.

This too is being done at considerable, as yet largely unrecognised, cost. The American Department of Agriculture estimated in 1986 that a quarter of all irrigated land was causing the underground water table to drop by from 10 cm to 1 metre per year. In the short term this type of exploitation can provide answers but in the long term it is clear that only what is replenished can be used each year. A very old law of nature.

This same fall in the water tables is matched in Africa, India and China. Ground water is being used at a rate that cannot be sustained by replenishment from the rain. And at the same time the demands from rapidly growing cities with water-consuming industries ensure that surface water is in short supply around the world.

Human ingenuity will solve many of these problems, but in what timescale, and at what cost? New irrigation technologies will boost the efficient use of water, but many countries will have difficulty in maintaining even the existing irrigation systems against the competition for water from growing human numbers and the demands of industrialisation.

Protecting the soil

At the Mauna Loa Observatory in Hawaii, scientists can detect within days when ploughing starts in North China. They discover this by analysing the soil particles which come from the start of the ploughing season which coincides with a period of low rainfall and high winds in the semi-arid regions of North Asia.

The depositing of this Asian soil in the South Pacific is but one example of the damage being done to the system which supports the agriculture of the world. The World Bank suggests that the gradual losses of agricultural production from soil erosion and degradation could translate into annual losses of farm output of between .5 % to 1.5 %.

Hundreds of abandoned settlements across the Sahelian belt of Africa bear witness to the fact that there is not enough topsoil left to support any food producing crops. And in the irrigated lands of the world the situation is no more reassuring. Approximately one tenth of all irrigated land is suffering from salinisation severe enough to affect yields, while another 30% is suffering from salinisation to a lesser extent.

We therefore seem to have a system where science and technology can offer monitoring of what is happening to the earth of a very high standard. We know what seems to be going wrong, but are locked into systems which seem to make it impossible for us to take precautionary action.

We are like a motorist who comes around a bend at night and sees what he thinks is a child in the middle of the road and responds by removing his spectacles to check whether there is a smudge on the glass, then sends for a sociologist to interview the parents to discover what family shortcomings have led to their child wandering unaccompanied on the road, then sends for a mathematician to calculate the trajectory of the child after impact with the car. The most obvious action, to slam on the brakes, seems to be impossible. The one necessary action is a precautionary one... a child may be on the road, I must stop.

Why is it that as a group we find it so difficult to slam on the brakes? What happens to the instinct of the individual when one becomes a group?

The greatest problem to me seems to be the failure to understand connections and the interconnectedness of all the elements in nature. Decisions are made without the knowledge of a greater design, of subtle interactions, of counter currents.

And most decisions are made with the best intentions in the world.

The tomato as economic metaphor

Consider the humble tomato that the average American buys in his supermarket. Consider the process by which the tasteless hard bright red tomato gets into the supermarket. (I'm indebted to an article in 'Farm and Food Research' for this information.)

The seed of this unblemished uniform bright red tomato is a hybrid owned and patented by Calgene Inc. They purchased it from the University of California at Davis where it was developed with research grants of American taxpayer's money. Before planting, the seeds are treated with mercury from Monsanto (the multi-national corporation) to ensure high germination. Some of this mercury remains in the soil and some is absorbed into the plants.

The Mexican Development Corporation, funded by taxpayers in Mexico, assisted the Jolly Green Giant Company to purchase the land from peasant farmers who have been turned into day labourers paid $2.50 a day... not enough to feed their families.

Before starting to plant, the fields (hundreds of acres in size) are fumigated with methyl bromide to kill potential pests of tomatoes. This chemical is made by CF Industries and is far more destructive to the ozone layer than CFC's. A chemical fertilizer (made by Cargill) which destroys millions of beneficial micro-organisms per square inch is added to the soil with the seeds.

Now this kind of monoculture, which eliminates natural diversity, requires massive doses of pesticides and herbicides.

These are provided by Union Carbide.

The farm labourers handle these chemicals without masks or gloves and few have access to health care or careful instruction on using these toxic chemicals.

The tomato is then picked green and placed in a plastic tray covered by plastic wrapping, then packed in a cardboard box. The plastic is made with petrochemicals and chlorine by the Formosa Company. Their workers and the residents in the area of Point Comfort in Texas, suffer from significantly higher than average rates of cancer and birth defects due to dioxin exposure which is a byproduct of the manufacturing process. The cardboard for the boxes is made from the wood of 300 year old trees growing in British Columbia and is processed in a mill on Lake Ontario where residents are warned not to eat the contaminated fish.

The boxed tomato is then gassed in ethylene chlorohydrin made by American Cyanamid in order to turn it red, and is sent by refrigerated truck to a warehouse. The truck and the warehouse are temperature controlled with CFC coolants made by Dupont.

After the harvest the plants are ploughed back into the soil along with the pesticide residues. After several years of drenching the soil with chemicals, it becomes so depleted of natural nutrients and organisms that it is virtually dead, and when the harvest declines appreciably, the corporation simply moves on to other fields.

All that remains is ruined fields, ruined local economy and ruined lives.

Now one could follow this process into the supermarket and the home revealing at every step complex linkages with business, industry, government and consumers. And at every step of the way from seed to consumption, good intentions, based on limited criteria for decision making, are the hallmark.

It is not my intention here to apportion blame. … what I wish to illustrate is the extraordinarily complex nature of the life that the privileged people of the earth have made for themselves in the name of convenience and choice, for it seems to me that ultimately the consumer society is almost certain to bring those 'very desirable' things to an end. And this ultimately comes down to a lack of accountability from the institutions set up to deal with these issues. Corporate Agribusiness, heavy and light industry, central and local government can in this way destroy soil fertility, environmental diversity, rural economies and the nutrient content of the food supplies of the very privileged on whose behalf these developments take place.

What then are the solutions? People authorised their governments to do these things. Only people can reverse these trends, for when you buy a tomato produced in this way, you support the system that created it. Yet ordinary people believe that they lack the power to do anything about it.

The role of Education

At this point I return to the Cairo Conference which I mentioned at the beginning of this talk. Out of this conference came the extraordinary goal of stabilising human numbers at 8 to 9 billion by the middle of the next century.

Literacy, particularly female literacy, it is suggested, will be the means by which this target can be achieved, and if this is the case then there is indeed some cause for cautious optimism. There are already encouraging indications that a number of African countries are at a critical turning point. Total fertility rates have already fallen in Botswana (6.9 in 1965 to 4.7 in 1990), Zimbabwe (8.0 in 1965 to 4.9 in 1990) and Kenya (8.0 in 1965 to 6.5 in 1990). There are also indications of decline in Ghana, Sudan and Togo.

Education has matched these improvements. Over 80% of children of the relevant age are enrolled in primary schools in developing countries. And in the newly industrialised countries of South East Asia some 90% of pupils of the appropriate age are enrolled in secondary schools.

We are all tied to ways of living by social conventions that have evolved over centuries. They arise out of our relationship with our families and friends, our faith, our schooling, the stories we are told, our cultural activities and increasingly by newspapers, radio and television.

These are the things that educate us through our lives, make us the people we are, create the rich diversity of our cultures and determine the way we view, relate to and use the environment. And this diversity is valuable, in my opinion, beyond words.

And if this rich diversity is to be retained then all these sectors of the educational process need to take on responsibility for improving the quality of decision making about the use of the resources of the earth and our interaction with the environment.

This is important, not just for the environment but for education as well. One of its prime functions is to prepare people for the opportunities, responsibilities and experiences they will face though their lives. Among the most important are the way in which they will interact with the environment.

Many people spend their whole lives directly managing and using the environment, seeking out or catching food, gathering fuel, collecting water and building their shelter from what they find about them. They traditionally receive an education that prepares them for their own land management roles. But the influences from outside their cultures ensure that this education is no longer sufficient.

It is less easy for people who work in offices, factories or the home to perceive their impact on the environment even though it influences their health and sense of well being.

They find it difficult to link the exhaust fumes of their cars to a rise in sea level caused by global warming; difficult to link a loss of species diversity in sub-tropical grasslands to the food they buy in the supermarkets; difficult to link the water they use to the decline of lowland wetlands so important to birds or the flooding of mountain valleys by dams and reservoirs. Their education often has little relevance to their environmental roles or responsibilities. As teachers, all of us, do we believe that the education we offer, whether formal or informal, has this relevance?

It is hard for individuals in a complex society to make a direct impact on decisions about the environment made by people in government and industry who they do not know and who have access to information, authority and spheres of influence to which they have no access.

So everyone needs and has a right to an environmental component to all the education they receive. Everyone is entitled to experiences which will enable them to understand, analyse and respond to the environmental problems they meet throughout their lives.

In conclusion

I started out speaking about the linear way in which much thinking takes place in the privileged world. Decisions are made, based largely on technical information and lack any clear notion of ultimate responsibility.

But what seems to me to be clear is that if one cuts down a single tree in the centre of a forest, waves of change will move outward from that tree as surely as if one had dropped a stone into a still pond.

Humans must learn to recognise this interconnectedness with nature in everything that they do. The teachings of the rich and various faith communities, which have throughout history pursued a holistic view of humanity, are needed now more than at any time.

CRACKING IT

after Arthur Dahl, UNEP

You talk of how science and technology have changed
The context of our religions –
And how, in this world, it's only cash that counts
And in the strain, on the rack, of that
The family is weakened (that is, *all* of us)
Overpopulation overloads our earth-home –
And we have refugees who have no hope

There are the things we know (as your voice slows)
And the things that 'no one wants to talk about'
The free movement, not of money, but of people
That have the right to be – imagine – world citizens
In the oneness that all this breaking down is for:

And without it, as you lift the lid, the shadow swarms:
Rats, like us, who don't have the space
Running over, and maiming, and mounting each other...
Rats in the subways of New York and London
Those cornered creatures we want to kill,

While they perform our nightmare for us –
And do we plan, or drift on till some catastrophe overwhelms us?

The catastrophe is here: this sickness at the root
Is all we have denied, and deny in our lives
IT IS THE SHADOW THAT WILL DROWN US

And draw us down
To where the only change can come: from the bottom up,

Under the manhole cover of our minds.

Jay Ramsay

FROM THE ALCOVE
after Andrew Steer, World Bank

Somewhere between Christ and Lucifer
With your silver-grey hair and quicksilver tongue
As you slide the transparencies over each other –
Mercurial in the projector's glow, and your shadow,
As your rapid polished monologue lulls us

Into believing – into hoping, even
Beyond the figures you skate over like thinning ice
Smiling – energized – as you arabesque and spin
And stop dead with your hand outstretched to grasp:

And I could, we could all almost vote for you now
For the Father Of Comfort And Finance And Light,
Making us feel as safe and secure as we need…
And it's not that I don't believe you
– or see how easy it is for us to distrust you –
Everything you say is right on and good: it stands

It's just that He is crucified everywhere on earth,
Where you arrive with your plans and panaceas –
It's just that you can't serve two masters
Without being bought, or sold

Even as we need these doors to open

And still it's true, as we used to say
(When we could see no way beyond the paradox)
'Deal in the market place, but always with true gold'.*

*alchemical saying, 17th c.

Jay Ramsay

THE RIDDLE OF DEVELOPMENT
after Dominick Harrod

We leave the library, and I walk out
Not knowing the answers to anything –

And as I let go, something clears as I glance down
At the verges of the grass lit green in the sun,
As it comes:

Is it a child examining a ladybird
Or a ladybird looking up at a child ?

Is it a child exterminating ants
Or letting them file by under his eyes ?

What does it mean, to help or interfere ?

Surely, to feel first is everything
And to hold the world in our hands as we are held

And then to know – if we close our eyes –
What holds and guides our greater minds.

Jay Ramsay

THE PRACTICE OF CONSERVATION BY RELIGIONS
Martin Palmer
ICOREC

O NE DAY in 1953 two men stood on the summit of Mount Everest, Sir Edmund Hillary, a Western scientist and Sherpa Tenzing, a Himalayan Buddhist. Separated as they were by culture and beliefs, they had together scaled the highest mountain in the world and had, for the first time in history, reached its summit. What they then did speaks volumes for the real differences between them and their cultures. Edmund Hillary stuck a Union Jack, the flag of Great Britain, in the snow and claimed to have 'conquered' Mt Everest. Sherpa Tenzing sank to his knees and asked forgiveness of the gods of the mountain for having disturbed them.

When the newspapers of the West reported this event, they all took up the 'conquered' theme. Not one saw anything to report in the prayers which were offered.

Some thirty years on Edmund Hillary commented that perhaps Sherpa Tenzing had more fully understood what was happening than he did. Everest, like the rest of the Himalayas, is in a desperate state. Invasion of its peaks in the last few decades has resulted in massive logging, pollution, and destruction of fragile habitats. The UK government has just sent a team to remove the 10 tons of rubbish left on the higher sections of the mountain by climbers.

Yet this is a sacred mountain to the local people, who for millennia have lived in a more balanced relationship with that mountain.

A material view and a spiritual view. One proclaims that a man who might live for 90 maybe 100 years, can 'conquer' a mountain some 50–60 million years old – a mountain that will still be here when *Homo Sapiens* has become extinct. The other, a view of human beings as just part of something much, much greater.

In trying to understand the practice of conservation by religions, it is insights such as these which we need to notice, as much as the actual, 'hands on projects' which so many religious organisations now run on conservation.

We all inhabit worlds created by beliefs. If I believe that human beings are the only important species on earth and that I need care nothing for the future, then I will use, or abuse the environment in one way. If however I believe that the world is an inter-connected web of life in which the human being is but a small part, then I will use or relate to the rest of the natural world in a very different way. What we do is conditioned by what we believe. It is as basic as that. Put quite simply, the environmental crisis is a crisis of the mind and the imagination and of beliefs, not a crisis of nature itself.

Therefore, no matter how much information or data we supply, if we have a world view which views the world as something there just for us, our action and interpretation will reflect that world view. Let me give an example.

The first really major international gathering on the environment under UN auspices was the Stockholm Conference of 1972. At that conference, vast amounts of data were provided by scientific organisations and conservation groups, hoping to persuade the leaders of the world's nations to take the decline of the environment seriously.

One particular area of concern was the rise in the destruction of the tropical rainforests. Scientists and environmentalists presented a terrible picture of the loss of these vital eco-systems. They told of nations selling off their forests for cash rather than preserving them for posterity. The intention in the minds of those presenting the information was to shock others by this catalogue of destruction.

But what happened at the receiving end was rather different. Some leaders of delegations, especially from countries struggling with debt burdens and massive poverty amongst their people, as well as some leaders of delegations from corrupt governments, heard something different. They heard that people out there in the commercial world would pay good, hard currency for the useless forests in the badlands of their countries.

The result? The rate of destruction of the rainforests leapt upwards after Stockholm. It is not information that will change the world. It is a world view which can use that information within a wider ethical, moral, and spiritual ethos.

This is what religions bring to conservation. At Assisi five of the world's major faiths for the first time ever clearly and unambiguously stated their position on the environment. The four faiths which have joined since Assisi have done likewise. The Declarations made by these faiths shows that all the faiths have fundamental teachings about why we should care for the environment.

Sadly however, little was being done by the faiths ten years ago to give life and meaning to these teachings. To some extent this was because they had been forgotten, or glossed over. Sometimes it was because the faith itself had become caught up in other modes of thinking which blunted the message of care for creation. Or social and economic forces had so penetrated their culture with a vision of the consumerist lifestyle, that the old teachings were ignored by many as being out of date or irrelevant.

When WWF issued its challenge to the faiths to make their teachings real in the struggle to save the natural world, few could have foreseen the scale of the response. Some undertook a fundamental assessment of what their faith should be doing officially on conservation – such as the Bahá'ís and some of the branches of the Christian faith like the Orthodox Church. Others began to realise that they had been practising passive conservation for centuries, through the influence of holy sites, mountains and temples. For example, Buddhism and Hinduism offer sanctuaries for endangered species by the simple fact that people do not log, hunt or trap on sacred land.

An example of this from Islam is that in the city of Istanbul which has grown from one million to eleven million in twenty or so years, the only remaining breeding site for storks is in the grounds of the Mosque of Eyup. Here, gravestones cover the hillside and the trees, which once covered all this area, survive only in the graveyard and mosque precincts. Without them, the storks of Istanbul would be history.

Yet others have begun to rediscover their teachings and to look afresh at their own lifestyles. The Jain programme to apply the principle of *ahimsa* – non-violence, with renewed insight to Jain business practices, has led to shifts in behaviour and in investment in line with traditional Jain practices.

But perhaps the most important way in which religions practise conservation is one which it is almost impossible to quantify. It does not manifest itself in grand schemes, nor in long papers. It is not presented to international conferences and does not figure in the assessments of political or economic leaders. It is presented through teaching, music, dance, festival and fasting, through sacred texts and prayers, liturgy and meditation, through song and silence. It is the vision of our place within a greater order; a sense of being part of a Divine purpose, however that is understood. It is the feeling of community with each other and with the rest of creation; the inspiration that we gain from an understanding of the wonder and glory of all creation.

These may seem to the hard-nosed scientist, the over-worked economist or the stressed-out conservationist, to be vague even sanctimonious ideals. Yet for millions upon millions of people throughout history and to this very day, it is through the songs of their faith, the festivals and fasts of their calendar, the rituals of their life-cycle that an understanding and relationship with the Divine, with themselves and with nature has been communicated.

Practical programmes are important. But they are fundamentally flawed unless there is the will, the vision and the belief in them to make them not just work, but become part of one's being. The most exciting thing about the rising tide of religious involvement in conservation is that increasingly it is becoming impossible to call oneself a person of faith without this having consequences for one's attitude towards nature. It is this which in the long term offers more hope than any number of reports and surveys of what is happening to nature.

Following the successful Summit on Religions and Conservation, conceived by Dr. Terumichi Kawai and made possible by the generosity and support of President Kawai and MOA International, we need to keep the dynamic balance between the practical and the inspirational. We need to keep the tension between the information which science can offer and the meaning which religions can provide. We need to strive to push for more and more work by the faiths, but not at the cost of losing the reflective and educational aspects of the religions.

When we started this work in 1986, we saw it as a mutual challenge. We saw the conservationists challenging the religions to make real their profound teachings. But we also saw the faiths questioning whether the secular conservation world has really understood what motivates people. That dialogue continues to this day. It is this challenge that the Alliance of Religions and Conservation – ARC – has been established to respond to. The creation of a new fund to assist the faiths in becoming more involved in conservation.

As a Christian, I believe in hope. I believe that people can change. If I did not, then I could not work on conservation. If I believed we were doomed by our greed and selfishness, I think I would curl up in a corner and die. It is because I believe in redemption, liberation, change – call it what you will – that I can continue to work in this area.

Perhaps this is the greatest thing that religions bring to the practice of conservation – hope. Hope that we can change, rediscover our truths and then journey on together, each in our own ways, but side by side, towards a world in which the whole of life is loved, respected and appreciated. For this is a truth that we all can find within our own traditions and even within our own hearts.

PART TWO

Faith Statements on Ecology

SECTION I

THE ASSISI DECLARATIONS

IN THE late summer of 1986, an historic event occurred in the Umbrian hilltown of Assisi. For the first time, representatives of the great faiths of the world came together in pilgrimage in order to hear what religion had to offer to conservation and what conservation had to share with religion.

Pilgrims, religious leaders, musicians and dancers marched into Assisi alongside scientists and conservationists, their divisions overcome by their shared commitment to the natural world. As they entered the town, the marchers were met by a glorious cacophony of sound and colour as singers and performers from many different parts of the world joined in their joyful celebrations.

The following day, 800 people gathered in the Basilica of St. Francis of Assisi to participate in an inspiring ceremony, at which representatives of five great religions, the WWF family, the pilgrims and many other guests affirmed their commitment to safeguarding the integrity of creation.

As Father Serrini, Minister General of the Franciscans said in his introduction:

> We are convinced of the inestimable value of our respective traditions and of what they can offer to re-establish ecological harmony; but, at the same time, we are humble enough to desire to learn from each other. The very richness of our diversity lends strength to our shared concern and responsibility for our Planet Earth.

The final part of the Assisi celebrations, which shifted the focus from the present to the future, was the issuing of the Declarations. These are the authoritative statements on ecology and nature from the five major faiths – Buddhism, Christianity, Hinduism, Islam and Judaism – sections of which are reprinted below.

Leaders of the faiths have since sought to put what they had learned into practice through practical conservation projects and programmes of environmental education. A vast number of such projects are now operating throughout the world, ensuring that the ecological message reaches millions of people.

Soon after Assisi, three more faiths – Bahá'i, Jainism and Sikhism – produced their own Declarations to accompany those of the other religions and these are also shown below. The significance of Assisi was summed up by HRH The Duke of Edinburgh, when he announced during the ceremony that, 'a new and powerful alliance has been forged between the forces of religion and the forces of conservation.'

EXTRACTS FROM THE ASSISI DECLARATIONS

Buddhism

There is a natural relationship between a cause and its resulting consequences in the physical world. In the life of the sentient beings too, including animals, there is a similar relationship of positive causes bringing about happiness, while undertakings generated through ignorance and negative attitude bring about suffering and misery. And this positive human attitude is, in the final analysis, rooted in genuine and unselfish compassion and loving kindness that seeks to bring about light and happiness for all sentient beings. Hence Buddhism is a religion of love, understanding and compassion, and committed towards the ideal of non-violence. As such, it also attaches great importance to wild life and the protection of the environment on which every being in this world depends for survival.

*

We regard our survival as an undeniable right. As co-inhabitants of this planet, other species too have this right for survival. And since human beings as well as other non-human sentient beings depend upon the environment as the ultimate source of life and wellbeing, let us share the conviction that the conservation of the environment, the restoration of the imbalance caused by our negligence in the past, be implemented with courage and determination.

Christianity

God declared everything to be good, indeed, very good. He created nothing unnecessarily and has omitted nothing that is necessary. Thus, even in the mutual opposition of the various elements of the universe, there exists a divinely willed harmony because creatures have received their mode of existence by the will of their Creator, whose purpose is that through their interdependence they should bring to perfection the beauty of the universe. It is the very nature of things considered in itself, without regard to man's convenience or inconvenience, that gives glory to the Creator.

*

Man's dominion cannot be understood as licence to abuse, spoil, squander or destroy what God has made to manifest his glory. That dominion cannot be anything other than a stewardship in symbiosis with all creatures. On the one hand, man's position verges on a viceregal partnership with God; on the other, his self-mastery in symbiosis with creation must manifest the Lord's exclusive and absolute dominion over everything, over man and his stewardship. At the risk of destroying himself, man may not reduce to chaos or disorder, or, worse still, destroy God's bountiful treasures.

*

Every human act of irresponsibility towards creatures is an abomination. According to its gravity, it is an offence against that divine wisdom which sustains and gives purpose to the interdependent harmony of the universe.

Hinduism

Hinduism believes in the all encompassing sovereignty of the divine, manifesting itself in a graded scale of evolution. The human race, though at the top of the evolutionary pyramid at present, is not seen as something apart from the earth and its multitudinous lifeforms.

*

The Hindu viewpoint on nature is permeated by a reverence for life, and an awareness that the great forces of nature – the earth, the sky, the air, the water and fire – as well as various orders of life including plants, and trees, forests and animals, are all bound to each other within the great rhythms of nature. The divine is not exterior to creation, but expresses itself through natural phenomena. In the Mudaka Upanishad the divine is described as follows:

> fire is his head, his eyes are the moon and sun;
> the regions of space are his ears, his voice the revealed Veda;
> the wind is his breath, his heart is the entire universe;
> the earth is his footstool, truly he is the inner soul of all.

*

The natural environment has received the close attention of the ancient Hindu scriptures. Forests and groves were considered sacred, and flowering trees received special reverence. Just as various animals were associated with gods and goddesses, different trees and plants were also associated in the Hindu pantheon. The Mahabharata says that 'even if there is only one tree full of flowers and fruits in a village, that place becomes worthy of worship and respect.'

Islam

The essence of Islamic teachings is that the entire universe is God's creation. Allah makes the waters flow upon the earth, upholds the heaven, makes the rain fall and keeps the boundaries between day and night. The whole of the rich and wonderful universe belongs to God, its maker. It is God who created the plants and the animals in their pairs and gave them the means to multiply. Then God created mankind – a very special creation because mankind alone was created with reason and the power to think and even the means to turn against the Creator. Mankind has the potential to acquire a status higher than that of the angels or sink lower than the lowliest of the beasts.

*

For the Muslim, mankind's role on earth is that of a *khalifa*, viceregent or trustee of God. We are God's stewards and agents on Earth. We are not masters of this Earth, it does not belong to us to do what we wish. It belongs to God and He has entrusted us with its safekeeping. Our function as viceregents, *khalifa* of God, is only to oversee the trust. The *khalifa* is answerable for his/her actions, for the way in which he/she uses or abuses the trust of God.

*

Allah is Unity; and His Unity is also reflected in the unity of humanity, and the unity of mankind and nature. His trustees are responsible for maintaining the unity of His creation, the integrity of the Earth, its flora and fauna, its wildlife and natural environment. Unity cannot be had by discord, by setting one need against another or letting one end predominate over another; it is maintained by balance and harmony.

Judaism

When God created the world, so the Bible tells us, He made order out of primal chaos. The sun, the moon, and the stars, plants, animals, and ultimately man, were each created with a rightful and necessary place in the universe. They were not to encroach on each other. 'Even the divine teaching, the Torah, which was revealed from on high, was given in a set measure' (*Vayikra Rabbah* 15:22) and even these holy words may not extend beyond their assigned limit.

*

The highest form of obedience to God's commandments is to do them not in mere acceptance but in the nature of union with Him. In such a joyous encounter between man and God, the very rightness of the world is affirmed. The encounter of God and man in nature is thus conceived in Judaism as a seamless web with man as the leader and custodian of the natural world.

*

There is a tension at the centre of the Biblical tradition, embedded in the very story of creation itself, over the question of power and stewardship. The world was created because God willed it, but why did He will it? Judaism has maintained, in all of its versions, that this world is the arena that God created for man, half beast and half angel, to prove that he could behave as a moral being. The Bible did not fail to demand even of God Himself that He be bound, as much as man, by the law of morality. Thus Abraham stood before God, after He announced that He was about to destroy the wicked city of Sodom, and Abraham demanded of God Himself that He produce moral justification for this act:

'Shall not the judge of all the earth do justice?' Comparably, man was given dominion over nature, but he was commanded to behave towards the rest of creation with justice and compassion. Humanity lives, always, in tension between his power and the limits set by conscience.

Bahá'í (1987)

Nature in its essence is the embodiment of My Name, the Maker, the Creator. Its manifestations are diversified by varying causes, and in this diversity there are signs for men of discernment. Nature is God's Will and is its expression in and through the contingent world. It is a dispensation of Providence ordained by the Ordainer, the All-Wise. (*Bahá'í Writings*)

With those words, Bahá'u'lláh, Prophet-Founder of the Bahá'í Faith, outlines the essential relationship between man and the environment: that the grandeur and diversity of the natural world are purposeful reflections of the majesty and bounty of God. For Bahá'ís, there follows an implicit understanding that nature is to be respected and protected, as a divine trust for which we are answerable.

*

As the most recent of God's revelations, however, the Bahá'í teachings have a special relevance to present-day circumstances when the whole of nature is threatened by man-made perils ranging from the wholesale destruction of the world's rain forests to the final nightmare of nuclear annihilation.

A century ago, Bahá'u'lláh proclaimed that humanity has entered a new age. Promised by all the religious Messengers of the past, this new epoch will ultimately bring peace and enlightenment for humanity. To reach that point, however, humankind must first recognize its fundamental unity – as well as the unity of God and of religion. Until there is a general recognition of this wholeness and interdependence, humanity's problems will only worsen.

Jainism (1991)

The Jain ecological philosophy is virtually synonymous with the principle of *ahimsa* (non-violence) which runs through the Jain tradition like a golden thread.

Ahimsa is a principle that Jains teach and practise not only towards human beings but towards all nature. It is an unequivocal teaching that is at once ancient and contemporary.

*

There is nothing so small and subtle as the atom nor any element so vast as space. Similarly, there is no quality of soul more subtle than non-violence and no virtue of spirit greater than reverence for life.

*

The teaching of *ahimsa* refers not only to wars and visible physical acts of violence but to violence in the hearts and minds of human beings, their lack of concern and compassion for their fellow humans and for the natural world. Ancient Jain texts explain that violence (*himsa*) is not defined by actual harm, for this may be unintentional. It is the intention to harm, the absence of compassion, that makes action violent. Without violent thought there could be no violent actions.

*

Jain cosmology recognises the fundamental natural phenomenon of symbiosis or mutual dependence. All aspects of nature belong together and are bound in a physical as well as a metaphysical relationship. Life is viewed as a gift of togetherness, accommodation and assistance in a universe teeming with interdependent constituents.

Sikhism (1989)

Since the beginning of the Sikh religion in the late 15th century, the faith has been built upon the message of the 'oneness of Creation'. Sikhism believes the universe was created by an almighty God. He himself is the creator and the master of all forms in the universe, responsible for all modes of nature and all elements in the world.

*

Sikhism firmly believes God to be the source of birth, life and death of all beings. God is the omniscient, the basic cause of the creation and the personal God of them all.

> From the Divine command occurs the creation and the dissolution of the universe. (p. 117 *Guru Granth Sahib*)

*

As their creator, the natural beauty, which exists and can be found in all living things whether animals, birds, fish, belongs to Him and He alone is their master and without His Hukum (order) nothing exists, changes or develops.

Having brought the world into being, God sustains, nourishes and protects it. Nothing is overlooked. Even creatures in rocks and stones are well provided for. Birds who fly thousands of miles away leaving their young ones behind know that they would be sustained and taught to fend for themselves by God (Guru Arjan, in Rehras). The creatures of nature lead their lives under God's command and with God's grace.

THE WINDSOR STATEMENTS

*T*HE DECLARATIONS which resulted from Assisi were the start of a continuing process of reflection and action on ecological issues by each of the major faiths. In 1995, representatives of these faiths came together once more for a Summit of Religions and Conservation at Windsor Castle.

The eight religions – Bahá'ís, Buddhists, Christians, Hindus, Jains, Jews, Muslims and Sikhs – which had been involved previously were joined at this stage by the Taoists. Over three days, they met with conservation organisations and other interested bodies such as the World Bank, to discuss the spiritual and ethical resources within religion that promote and encourage care for creation.

At the Summit, each faith presented an action plan for environmental work over the next nine years. A new foundation – the Alliance of Religions and Conservation (ARC) – was established to co-ordinate the various practical and educational projects undertaken by each religion.

The representatives of each religion also drafted new and more detailed statements of their position on faith and ecology, to highlight the deepening understanding that had developed through this process of reflection and dialogue. This section contains extracts from these statements.

Each faith statement is preceded by a poem by Jay Ramsay, a personal reflection on what each religious leader said and the truths and insights contained therein.

BAHÁ'Í

for Madame Rabbani and Lawrence Arturo

Start at the beginning –
Start with the Oneness we all knew
Lying out in a pure shaft of green-dappled sunlight
Where you were one with the light and the grass.

This is the Day Of the Child

    This is the day of the child before time –

        When we were together in the light, before Christ.

This is the day that has come now:
Where we return to a Garden that is feeling before speech,
That is Paradise, gold, in our cells.

And when we remember what we've always known
All we can do and be can be healing.

Tell the children. Teach the children to teach us,
For theirs is the kingdom we have poisoned with our minds.

Jay Ramsay

THE BAHÁ'Í FAITH
The Bahá'í Teachings on Conservation and Sustainable Development

IN THIS AGE of transition toward a world society, protection of the environment and conservation of the earth's resources represent an enormously complex challenge. The rapid progress in science and technology that has united the world physically has also greatly accelerated destruction of the biological diversity and rich natural heritage with which the planet has been endowed. Material civilisation, driven by the dogmas of consumerism and aggressive individualism and disoriented by the weakening of moral standards and spiritual values, has been carried to excess.

Only a comprehensive vision of a global society, supported by universal values and principles, can inspire individuals to take responsibility for the long-term care and protection of the natural environment. Bahá'ís find such a world-embracing vision and system of values in the teachings of Bahá'u'lláh – teachings which herald an era of planetary justice, prosperity and unity.

Bahá'u'lláh enjoins His followers to develop a sense of world citizenship and a commitment to stewardship of the earth. His writings are imbued with a deep respect for the natural world and for the interconnectedness of all things. They emphasise that the fruits of God's love and obedience to His commandments are dignity, nobility and a sense of worth. From these attributes emerge the natural inclination to treat one another with love and compassion, and the willingness to sacrifice for the betterment of society. Bahá'u'lláh also teaches moderation, a commitment to justice, and detachment from the things of this world – spiritual disciplines which enable individuals to contribute to the establishment of a prosperous and united world civilisation. The broad pattern for such a civilisation and the principles on which it should be based are set forth in Bahá'u'lláh's Revelation, a revelation which offers hope to a dispirited humanity and the promise that it is truly possible both to meet the needs of present and future generations and to build a sound foundation for social and economic development. The inspiration and the vision for this civilisation are captured in Bahá'u'lláh's words: 'The earth is but one country, and mankind its citizens.'[1]

Among the principles guiding the Bahá'í approach to conservation and sustainable development, the following are of particular importance:

- nature reflects the qualities and attributes of God and should, therefore, be greatly respected and cherished;
- all things are interconnected and flourish according to the law of reciprocity; and
- the oneness of humanity is the fundamental spiritual and social truth shaping our age.

Nature reflects the qualities and attributes of God.

Bahá'í Scriptures describe nature as an emanation of God's will:

> Nature in its essence is the embodiment of My Name, the Maker, the Creator. Its manifestations are diversified by varying causes, and in this diversity there are signs for men of discernment. Nature is God's Will and is its expression in and through the contingent world. It is a dispensation of Providence ordained by the Ordainer, the All-Wise.[2]

Understanding nature as a reflection of the majesty and an expression of the purpose of God inspires a deep respect for the natural world:

> Whatever I behold I readily discover that it maketh Thee known unto me, and it remindeth me of Thy signs, and of Thy tokens, and of Thy testimonies. By Thy glory! Every time I lift up mine eyes unto Thy heaven, I call to mind Thy highness and Thy loftiness, and Thine incomparable glory and greatness; and every time I turn my gaze to Thine earth, I am made to recognise the evidences of Thy power and the tokens of Thy bounty. And when I behold the sea, I find that it speaketh to me of Thy majesty, and of the potency of Thy might, and of Thy sovereignty and Thy grandeur. And at whatever time I contemplate the mountains, I am led to discover the ensigns of Thy victory and the standards of Thine Omnipotence.[3]

This attitude of respect is further reinforced by copious metaphorical references to the natural world woven throughout the Bahá'í Scriptures. However, while nature is greatly valued and respected, it is not to be worshipped or adored. Rather it is to serve the purpose given by God to the human race: to carry forward an ever-advancing civilisation. In this regard, the Bahá'í Faith promotes a world view that is neither bio-centric nor, strictly speaking, anthropocentric, but rather theocentric, with the Revelations of God at its centre. Humankind, as it strives to carry out the Divine Will in this, the physical realm, is thus the trustee or steward of nature.

1   Bahá'u'lláh, Gleanings from the Writings of Bahá'u'lláh. Wilmette: Bahá'í Publishing Trust, 1976, section CXVII, p. 250.
2   Bahá'u'lláh, from 'Tablet of Wisdom', published in Tablets of Bahá'u'lláh Revealed After the Kitáb-i-Aqdas (revised edition). Haifa: Bahá'í World Centre, 1982, p. 142.
3   Bahá'u'lláh, Prayers and Meditations by Bahá'u'lláh. Wilmette: Bahá'í Publishing Trust, 1987, section CLXXVI, p. 272.

Responsible stewardship of the natural world logically extends to the humane treatment of animals.

> It is not only their fellow human beings that the beloved of God must treat with mercy and compassion, rather must they show forth the utmost loving-kindness to every living creature.[4]

> Train your children from the earliest days to be infinitely tender and loving to animals.[5]

All things are interconnected and flourish according to the law of reciprocity. The principles of interconnectedness and reciprocity underlie the Bahá'í understanding of both the operations of the universe and the responsibilities of humankind.

> For every part of the universe is connected with every other part by ties that are very powerful and admit of no imbalance, nor any slackening whatever...[6]

> Co-operation and reciprocity are essential properties which are inherent in the unified system of the world of existence, and without which the entire creation would be reduced to nothingness.[7]

> Were one to observe with an eye that discovereth the realities of all things, it would become clear that the greatest relationship that bindeth the world of being together lieth in the range of created things themselves, and that cooperation, mutual aid and reciprocity are essential characteristics in the unified body of the world of being, inasmuch as all created things are closely related together and each is influenced by the other or deriveth benefit therefrom, either directly or indirectly.[8]

Evolutionary processes are explicitly affirmed in Bahá'í Scriptures:

> All beings, whether large or small, were created perfect and complete from the first, but their perfections appear in them by degrees. The organisation of God is one; the evolution of existence is one; the divine system is one... When you consider this universal system, you see that there is not one of the beings which at its coming into existence has reached the limit of perfection. No, they gradually grow and develop, and then attain the degree of perfection.[9]

The blessings of bio-diversity are also highlighted:

> Diversity is the essence of perfection and the cause of the appearance of the bestowals of the Most glorious Lord... This diversity, this difference is like the naturally created dissimilarity and variety of the limbs and organs of the human

4   'Abdu'l-Bahá, Selections from the Writings of 'Abdu'l-Bahá (revised edition). Haifa: Bahá'í World Centre, 1982, section 138, pp. 158–60.

5   'Abdu'l-Bahá, Selections from the Writings of 'Abdu'l-Bahá, section 138, pp. 158–60.

6   'Abdu'l-Bahá, Selections from the Writings of 'Abdu'l-Bahá, section 137, p. 157.

7   'Abdu'l-Bahá, from a previously untranslated Tablet.

8   'Abdu'l-Bahá, from a previously untranslated Tablet.

9   'Abdu'l-Bahá, Some Answered Questions. Wilmette: Bahá'í Publishing Trust, 1981 (reprint: 1982), p. 199.

> body, for each one contributeth to the beauty, efficiency and perfection of the whole… How unpleasing to the eye if all the flowers and plants, the leaves and blossoms, the fruits, the branches and the trees of that garden were all of the same shape and colour! Diversity of hues, form and shape, enricheth and adorneth the garden, and heighteneth the effect thereof…[10]

The spiritual and material planes are interconnected and act upon each other:

> We cannot segregate the human heart from the environment outside us and say that once one of these is reformed everything will be improved. Man is organic with the world. His inner life moulds the environment and is itself also deeply affected by it. The one acts upon the other and every abiding change in the life of man is the result of these mutual reactions.[11]

Given the fundamental unity of science and religion – the interconnectedness of the material and spiritual realms – it is not surprising that scientific pursuits are highly praised:

> The faculty of intellectual investigation into the secrets of creation… is the most praiseworthy power of man, for through its employment and exercise the betterment of the human race is accomplished, the development of the virtues of mankind is made possible…[12]

However, the exercise of the faculty of investigation must be guided by spiritual principles, especially moderation and humility:

> Any agency whatever, though it be the instrument of mankind's greatest good, is capable of misuse.[13]

> If carried to excess, civilisation will prove as prolific a source of evil as it had been of goodness when kept within the restraints of moderation.[14]

> Every man of discernment, while walking upon the earth, feeleth indeed abashed, inasmuch as he is fully aware that the thing which is the source of his prosperity, his wealth, his might, his exaltation, his advancement and power is, as ordained by God, the very earth which is trodden beneath the feet of all men. There can be no doubt that whoever is cognisant of this truth, is cleansed and sanctified from all pride, arrogance, and vainglory…[15]

In light of the interdependence and reciprocity of all parts of nature, the evolutionary perfection of all beings, and the importance of diversity 'to the beauty, efficiency and perfection of the whole,'[16] it is clear to Bahá'ís that, in the

---

10 'Abdu'l-Bahá, Selections from the Writings of 'Abdu'l-Bahá, section 225, p. 291.

11 Secretary of Shoghi Effendi, from a letter dated 17 February 1933 to an individual believer.

12 'Abdu'l-Bahá, Promulgation of Universal Peace: Talks Delivered by 'Abdu'l-Bahá during His Visit to the United States and Canada in 1912 (2nd edition). Wilmette: Bahá'í Publishing Trust, 1982, p. 31.

13 'Abdu'l-Bahá, The Secret of Divine Civilisation (2nd edition). Wilmette: Bahá'í Publishing Trust, 1983, p. 16.

14 Bahá'u'lláh, Gleanings from the Writings of Bahá'u'lláh, section CLXIV, p. 343.

15 Bahá'u'lláh, Epistle to the Son of the Wolf (revised edition). Wilmette: Bahá'í Publishing Trust, 1979, p. 44.

16 Abdu'l-Bahá, Selections from the Writings of 'Abdu'l-Bahá, section 225, p. 291.

ordering of human affairs, every effort should be made to preserve as much as possible the earth's bio-diversity and natural order.

Nevertheless, in the process of extending social and economic justice to the entire human family, certain difficult and possibly irreversible decisions may have to be taken. Such decisions, Bahá'ís believe, should be made within a consultative framework, involving those affected and taking into account the impact of any resulting policies, programmes and activities on the quality of life of subsequent generations.

For Bahá'ís, Bahá'u'lláh's promise that civilisation will exist on this planet for a minimum of five thousand centuries makes it unconscionable to ignore the long-term impact of decisions made today. The world community must, therefore, learn to make use of the earth's natural resources, both renewable and non-renewable, in a manner that ensures sustainability into the distant reaches of time. This does not, however, mean that Bahá'ís advocate a 'hands-off, back to the woods' policy. On the contrary, the world civilisation that Bahá'ís believe will eventually emerge will be animated by a deep religious faith and will be one in which science and technology will serve humanity and help it to live in harmony with nature.

The oneness of humanity is the fundamental spiritual and social truth shaping our age.

The oneness of humanity is, for Bahá'ís, the operating principle and ultimate goal of humankind's collective life on the planet. It is applicable not only to the individual, but also to the relationships that must bind all the states and nations as members of one human family:

> The oneness of mankind... implies an organic change in the structure of present-day society, a change such as the world has not yet experienced... It calls for no less than the reconstruction and the demilitarisation of the whole civilised world – a world organically unified in all the essential aspects of its life, its political machinery, its spiritual aspiration, its trade and finance, its script and language, and yet infinite in the diversity of the national characteristics of its federated units.[17]

> It represents the consummation of human evolution... and... carries with it no more and no less than a solemn assertion that attainment to this final stage in this stupendous evolution is not only necessary but inevitable, that its realisation is fast approaching, and that nothing short of a power that is born of God can succeed in establishing it.[18]

Bahá'í Scriptures maintain that adherence to the principle of the oneness of humanity will have a direct and enduring impact on man's spiritual, social and

---

17 Shoghi Effendi, The World Order of Bahá'u'lláh – Selected Letters. Wilmette: Bahá'í Publishing Trust, 1974 (revised edition), pp. 42–43.

18 Shoghi Effendi, The World Order of Bahá'u'lláh – Selected Letters, p. 43.

physical environments. Universal acceptance of this principle will entail a major restructuring of the world's educational, social, agricultural, industrial, economic, legal and political systems. This restructuring will facilitate the emergence of a sustainable, just and prosperous world civilisation. Ultimately only a spiritually based civilisation – in which science and religion work in harmony – will be able to preserve the ecological balance of the earth, foster stability in human population, and advance both the material and the spiritual well-being of all peoples and nations.

In Conclusion

Bahá'í Scriptures teach that, as trustees of the planet's vast resources and biological diversity, humanity must seek to protect the 'heritage [of] future generations;'[19] see in nature a reflection of the divine; approach the earth, the source of material bounties, with humility; temper its actions with moderation; and be guided by the fundamental spiritual truth of our age, the oneness of humanity. The speed and facility with which we establish a sustainable pattern of life will depend, in the final analysis, on the extent to which we are willing to be transformed, through the love of God and obedience to His Laws, into constructive forces in the process of creating an ever-advancing civilisation.

This statement was issued by the Bahá'í Office of the Environment on behalf of the Bahá'í International Community.

19   Shoghi Effendi, from a cable dated 23 May 1951 to the New Earth Luncheon, London, UK.

BUDDHISM

after the Venerable Kushok Bakula

'We all drink the same water of life', you say
With your quiet all-suffering, seeing face
Interpreted into our language –

And the leather brown of the earth of your skin
That is the contact of skin with the ground

Eyes that have seen all,
That know the pain and illusions we create,
And have let them go…to the earth and the sky

And isn't *this* tradition:
To return to what is alive
To what has always been here ?

So you named the mountain 'Ratna Peak'
You adjured abstention and compassion there –
And as you pause on the pass, in our eyes
You pray and ask forgiveness from it;

And the mountain is Divine.

And on the plains below, once tyranny* had collapsed –
The true faith grew up like flowering weeds, everywhere.

* Communism in Mongolia

Jay Ramsay

BUDDHISM

ALL BUDDHIST teachings and practice come under the heading of *Dharma* which means Truth and the path to Truth. The word *Dharma* also means 'phenomena' and in this way we can consider everything to be within the sphere of the teachings. All outer and inner phenomena, the mind and its surrounding environment are understood to be inseparable and interdependent. In his own lifetime the Buddha came to understand that the notion that one exists as an isolated entity is an illusion. All things are interrelated; we are interconnected and do not have autonomous existence. Buddha said, 'This is because that is; this is not because that is not; this is born because that is born; this dies because that dies'. The health of the whole is inseparably linked with the health of the parts, and the health of the parts is inseparably linked with the whole. Everything in life arises through causes and conditions.

Many Buddhist monks such as His Holiness the Dalai Lama, Venerable Thich Nhat Hanh, Venerable Kim Teng and Venerable Phra Phrachak emphasise the natural relationship between deep ecology and Buddhism. According to the Vietnamese monk Venerable Thich Nhat Hanh:

> Buddhists believe that the reality of the interconnectedness of human beings, society and Nature will reveal itself more and more to us as we gradually recover – as we gradually cease to be possessed by anxiety, fear and the dispersion of the mind. Among the three – human beings, society and Nature – it is us who begin to effect change. But in order to effect change we must recover ourselves, one must be whole. Since this requires the kind of environment favourable to one's healing, one must seek the kind of lifestyle that is free from the destruction of one's humaness. Efforts to change the environment and to change oneself are both necessary. But we know how difficult it is to change the environment if individuals themselves are not in a state of equilibrium.

In order to protect the environment we must protect ourselves. We protect ourselves by opposing selfishness with generosity, ignorance with wisdom, and hatred with loving kindness. Selflessness, mindfulness, compassion and wisdom are the essence of Buddhism. We train in Buddhist meditation which enables us to be aware of the effects of our actions, including those destructive to our environment. Mindfulness and clear comprehension are at the heart of Buddhist meditation. Peace is realised when we are mindful of each and every step.

In the words of Maha Ghosananda:

> When we respect the environment, then nature will be good to us. When our hearts are good, then the sky will be good to us. The trees are like our mother and father, they feed us, nourish us, and provide us with everything; the fruit, leaves, the branches, the trunk. They give us food and satisfy many of our needs. So we spread the *dharma* (truth) of protecting ourselves and protecting our environment, which is the dharma of the Buddha.

> When we accept that we are part of a great human family – that every being has the nature of Buddha – then we will sit, talk, make peace. I pray that this realisation will spread throughout our troubled world and bring humankind and the earth to its fullest flowering. I pray that all of us will realise peace in this lifetime and save all beings from suffering.

> The suffering of the world has been deep. From this suffering comes great compassion. Great compassion makes a peaceful heart. A peaceful heart makes a peaceful person. A peaceful person makes a peaceful family. A peaceful family makes a peaceful community. A peaceful community makes a peaceful nation. A peaceful nation makes a peaceful world. May all beings live in happiness and peace.

Buddhism as an Ecological Religion or a Religious Ecology

The relationship between Buddhist ideals and the natural world can be explored within three contexts:

1 Nature as Teacher
2 Nature as a Spiritual Force
3 Nature as a Way of Life

Nature as Teacher

> Like the Buddha, we too should look around us and be observant, because everything in the world is ready to teach us. With even a little intuitive wisdom we will be able to see clearly through the ways of the world. We will come to understand that everything in the world is a teacher. Trees and vines, for example can all reveal the true nature of reality. With wisdom there is no need to question anyone, no need to study. We can learn from Nature enough to be enlightened, because everything follows the way of Truth. It does not diverge from Truth. (*Ajahn Chah, Forest Sangha Newsletter*)

Buddha taught that respect for life and the natural world is essential. By living simply one can be in harmony with other creatures and learn to appreciate the interconnectedness of all that lives. This simplicity of life involves developing openness to our environment and relating to the world with awareness and responsive perception. It enables us to enjoy without possessing, and mutually benefit each other without manipulation.

However, the Buddha was no romantic idealist. He also saw and realised that all phenomena, including the natural world, was a pit of suffering. He saw creatures struggling for survival in a precarious world. He saw death and fear, the strong preying on the weak and the devastation of thousands of beings as one lonely figure ploughed the earth to reap the harvest. He also saw impermanence. As Ajahn Chah has written:

> take trees for example… first they come into being, then they grow and mature, constantly changing, until they finally die as every tree must. In the same way, people and animals are born, grow and change during their lifetimes until they eventually die. The multitudinous changes which occur during this transition from birth to death show the Way of *Dharma*. That is to say, all things are impermanent, having decay and dissolution as their natural condition. (*Buddha-Nature*)

Nature is not independent and unchanging and neither are we. Change is the very essence of nature. In the words of Stephen Batchelor :

> We each believe we are a solid and lasting self rather than a short term bundle of thoughts, feelings and impulses. (*The Sands of the Ganges*)

We do not exist independently, separate from everything else – all things in the universe come into existence, 'arise' as a result of particular conditions. It is surely a mistake to see fulfilment in terms of external or personal development alone.

Buddha taught us to live simply, to cherish tranquillity, to appreciate the natural cycle of life. In this universe of energies, everything affects everything else. Nature is an eco-system in which trees affect climate, the soil and the animals, just as the climate affects the trees, the soil, the animals and so on. The ocean, the sky, the air are all inter-related, and inter-dependent – water is life and air is life. A result of Buddhist practice is that one does not feel that one's existence is so much more important than anyone else's. The notions of ego clinging, the importance of the individual and emphasis on self is, in the West, a dominant outlook which is moving to the East as 'development' and consumerism spreads. Instead of looking at things as a seamless undivided whole we tend to categorise and compartmentalise. Instead of seeing nature as our great teacher we waste and do not replenish and forget that Buddha learned his 'Wisdom from Nature'.

Once we treat nature as our friend, to cherish it, then we can see the need to change from the attitude of dominating nature to an attitude of working with nature – we are an intrinsic part of all existence rather than seeing ourselves as in control of it.

Nature as a Spiritual Force

For Shantiveda in eighth century India, dwelling in nature was obviously preferable to living in a monastery or town:

> When shall I come to dwell in forests
> Amongst the deer, the birds and the trees,
> That say nothing unpleasant
> And are delightful to associate with.
> (*A Guide to the Bodhisattva's Way of Life*)

Patrul Rinpoche, one of the greatest Tibetan Buddhist teachers of the nineteenth century writes:

> Base your mind on the *Dharma*,
> Base your *Dharma* on a humble life,
> Base your humble life on the thought of death,
> Base your death on a lonely cave.
> (*The Words of my Perfect Teacher*)

The Buddha taught that the balance of nature is achieved by the functions of the forest. Survival of the forest is vital to the survival of natural harmony, balance, morality and environment.

Buddhist teachers and masters have constantly reminded us of the importance of living in tune with nature, to respect all life, to make time for meditation practice, to live simply and use nature as a spiritual force. Buddha stressed the four boundless qualities: loving-kindness, compassion, sympathetic joy (delight in the well-being of others) and equanimity (impartiality).

Venerable Asabho has spoken of the value of living in retreat in Hammer Woods, Chithurst. The forest has its own rhythms and after a few days the metabolism and sleeping patterns adjust and the senses begin to sharpen to this new and unfamiliar setting. Ear and nose play a more important role when not having any comforts of life – gas, electricity, artificial light and the like. Living in the fast and furious pace of the twentieth century our true nature is often dulled by the massive sensory impact unavoidable in modern urbanised living. Living close to nature is a very healing experience – to have few activities, few distractions. Learning to trust yourself and being more of a friend than a judge one develops a lightness of being, a light confidence. One realises the truth of the notion of impermanence – the sound of animals, the texture of trees, the subtle changes in the forest and land, the subtle changes in your own mind. Retreats, or simply living in the forest with nature:

> ... helps people get back to earth, to calm you down – just living with the unhurried rhythms of nature. With nature, everything – birth, growth, degeneration and decay is just as it is, and in that holistic sense everything is alright. Touching lightly is the right touch, the natural touch in which blame, praise, crises, retreats, progress, delays are just as it is and so all right.
> (*Talks given at Chithurst Buddhist Monastery*)

Living in this way we can appreciate the fragility of all we love, the fickleness of security. Retreat and solitude complement our religious practice and give the opportunity of deepening, refining and strengthening the mind. By being mindful about the daily routine one pays attention to the flow of life – to see nature as a positive, joyful, spiritual force.

Nature as a Way of Life

The Buddha commended frugality as a virtue in its own right. Skilful living avoids waste and we should try to recycle as much as we can. Buddhism advocates a simple, gentle, non-aggressive attitude towards nature – reverence for all forms of nature must be cultivated.

Buddha used examples from nature to teach – in his stories the plant and animal world are treated as part of our inheritance, even as part of ourselves (as Krishnamurti said 'we are the world, the world is us'). By starting to look at ourselves and the lives we are living we may come to appreciate that the real solution to the environmental crisis begins with us. Craving and greed only bring unhappiness – simplicity, moderation and the middle way bring liberation and hence equanimity and happiness. Our demands for material possessions can never be satisfied – we will always need to acquire more, there is not enough in the universe to truly satisfy us and give us complete satisfaction and contentment and no government can fulfil all our desires for security.

Buddhism, however, takes us away from the ethos of the individual and its bondage to materialism and consumerism. When we try to conquer greed and desire we can start to have inner peace and be at peace with those around us. The teaching of the Buddha, the reflections on *Dharma* relates to life as it actually is. To be mindful – receptive, open, sensitive and not fixed to any one thing but able to fix on things according to what is needed in that time and at that place.

By developing the right actions of not killing, stealing or misconduct in sexual desires perhaps we can begin to live with nature, without breaking it or injuring the rhythm of life. In our livelihoods by seeking work that does not harm other beings, refraining from trading in weapons, in breathing things, meat, alcohol and poisons we can feel more at one with nature.

Our minds can be so full, so hyper-active, we never allow ourselves a chance to slow down to be aware of our thoughts, feelings and emotions, to live fully in the present moment. We need to live as the Buddha taught us to live, in peace and harmony with nature but this must start with ourselves. If we are going to save this planet we need to seek a new ecological order, to look at the life we lead and then work together for the benefit of all; unless we work together no solution can be found. By moving away from self-centredness, to sharing wealth more, being more responsible for ourselves, and agreeing to live more simply,

we can help decrease much of the suffering in the world. As the Indian philosopher Nagarjuna said:

> ... things derive their being and nature by mutual dependence and are nothing
> in themselves.

> Breathing in, I know I'm breathing in,
> Breathing out, I know
> as the in-breath grows deep,
> the out-breath grows slow.
> Breathing in makes me calm.
> Breathing out makes me ease.
> With the in-breath, I smile.
> With the out-breath, I release.
> Breathing in, there is only the present moment
> Breathing out is a wonderful moment.
> (From a poem by Thich Nhat Hanh in *Buddhism and Ecology*)

This statement was written and edited by:
Kevin Fossey
Somdech Preah Maha Ghosananda
His Excellency Sri Kushok Bakula
Venerable Nhem Kim Teng

CHRISTIANITY

after Metropolitan John of Pergamon

'Brothers and sisters' – now, you address us as we are
As we were in the beginning –

A beginning we need to understand again:
We were given *dominion but not domination**
And all our long story has been
What we have fallen from, in separation

Because 'Creation is Beloved of God'
– the Earth and we are His Lover –
And hear this, the earth is not ours
'It is the Lord's – and then see what it becomes

See the ground and sky, and anything that moves as His,
And then realize we are guests here, honoured guests
Given the gift of our bodies we take
To know that God through us is one with us

And see how we have not seen this yet
This infusion of You in every particle...

We have dressed up and lived in our heads,
As you confess the damage we have done
Your voice echoing into the microphone

Where we need clear passionate speech, and a New Song.

* see *Genesis* 2:5

Jay Ramsay

CHRISTIANITY

CHRISTIANITY TEACHES that all of creation is the loving action of God who not only willed the creation but also continues to care for all aspects of existence. As Jesus says in the Gospel of Luke:

> Are not five sparrows sold for two pennies? Yet not one of them is forgotten by God. Indeed the very hairs of your head are all numbered. (Chapter 12, verses 6–7)

Yet sadly, many Christians have been more interested in the last part of what Jesus said:

> Don't be afraid, you are worth more than many sparrows.

There exists within Christianity a tension between God's creative, loving powers and humanity's capacity and tendency to rebel against God. Christianity, drawing upon the Biblical imagery of Genesis 1 and 2 and Genesis 9, is unambiguous about the special role of humanity within creation. But this special role has sometimes been interpreted as giving free rein to mastership. As the World Council of Churches said in the document from the Granvollen, Norway meeting of 1988:

> The drive to have 'mastery' over creation has resulted in the senseless exploitation of natural resources, the alienation of the land from people and the destruction of indigenous cultures... Creation came into being by the will and love of the Triune God, and as such it possesses an inner cohesion and goodness. Though human eyes may not always discern it, every creature and the whole creation in chorus bear witness to the glorious unity and harmony with which creation in endowed. And when our human eyes are opened and our tongues unloosed, we too learn to praise and participate in the life, love, power and freedom that is God's continuing gift and grace.

In differing ways, the main churches have sought to either revise or re-examine their theology and as a result their practice in the light of the environmental crisis. For example, Pope Paul VI in his Apostolic Letter, Octogesima Adventeins, also comments in a similar manner:

by an ill-considered exploitation of nature he [humanity] risks destroying it and becoming in his turn the victim of this degradation... flight from the land, industrial growth, continual demographic expansion and the attraction of urban centres bring about concentrations of population difficult to imagine.

In his New Year Message, 1990, His Holiness the Pope stated:

Christians, in particular, realise that their responsibility within creation and their duty towards nature and the Creator are an essential part of their faith.

In Orthodoxy this is brought out even more strongly, especially in the document produced by the Ecumenical Patriarchate, *Orthodoxy and the Ecological Crisis*, 1990. The Orthodox Church teaches that humanity, both individually and collectively, ought to perceive the natural order as a sign and sacrament of God. This is obviously not what happens today. Rather humanity perceives the natural order as an object of exploitation. There is no one who is not guilty of disrespecting nature, for to respect nature is to recognise that all creatures and objects have a unique place in God's creation. When we become sensitive to God's world around us, we grow more conscious also of God's world within us. Beginning to see nature as a work of God, we begin to see our own place as human beings within nature. The true appreciation of any object is to discover the extraordinary in the ordinary.

The Orthodox Church teaches that it is the destiny of humanity to restore the proper relationship between God and the world as it was in Eden. Through repentance, two landscapes – the one human, the other natural – can become the objects of a caring and creative effort. But repentance must be accompanied by soundly-focused initiatives which manifest the ethos of Orthodox Christian faith.

The World Council of Churches, predominantly Protestant, but also with full Orthodox participation, issued the following when they called their member churches together in 1990 to consider the issues of Justice, Peace and the integrity of Creation:

Affirmation VII

We affirm the creation as beloved of God.

We affirm that the world, as God's handiwork, has its own inherent integrity; that land, waters, air, forests, mountains and all creatures, including humanity, are 'good' in God's sight. The integrity of creation has a social aspect which we recognise as peace with justice, and an ecological aspect which we recognise in the self-renewing, sustainable character of natural ecosystems.

We will resist the claim that anything in creation is merely a resource for human exploitation. We will resist species extinction for human benefit;

consumerism and harmful mass production; pollution of land, air and waters; all human activities which are now leading to probable rapid climate change; and the policies and plans which contribute to the disintegration of creation.

Therefore we commit ourselves to be members of both the living community of creation in which we are but one species, and members of the covenant community of Christ; to be full co-workers with God, with moral responsibility to respect the rights of future generations; and to conserve and work for the integrity of creation both for its inherent value to God and in order that justice may be achieved and sustained.

Implicit in these affirmations is the belief that it has been human selfishness, greed, foolishness or even perversity that has wrought destruction and death upon so much of the planet. This is also central to Christian understanding. As far as we can tell, human beings are the only species capable of rebelling against what God has revealed as the way in which we should live. This rebellion takes many forms, but one of these is the abuse of the rest of creation. Christians are called to recognise their need to be liberated from those forces within themselves and within society which militate against a loving and just relationship one with another and between humans and the rest of creation. The need to repent for what has been done and to hope that change can really transform the situation are two sides of the same coin. The one without the other becomes defeatist or romantic – neither of which is ultimately of much use to the rest of the world.

The Orthodox Churches pursue this in their own line of theology and reflection concerning creation, and expressed their commitment in the document *Orthodoxy and the Ecological Crisis*, 1990:

> We must attempt to return to a proper relationship with the Creator AND the creation. This may well mean that just as a shepherd will in times of greatest hazard, lay down his life for his flock, so human beings may need to forego part of their wants and needs in order that the survival of the natural world can be assured. This is a new situation – a new challenge. It calls for humanity to bear some of the pain of creation as well as to enjoy and celebrate it. It calls first and foremost for repentance – but of an order not previously understood by many. (pp. 10–11)

The hope comes from a model of our relationship with nature which turns the power we so often use for destruction into a sacrificial or servant power – here using the image of the priest at the Eucharist:

> Just as the priest at the Eucharist offers the fullness of creation and receives it back as the blessing of Grace in the form of the consecrated bread and wine, to share with others, so we must be the channel through which God's grace and deliverance is shared with all creation. The human being is simply yet gloriously

the means for the expression of creation in its fullness and the coming of God's deliverance for all creation. (p. 8)

For Christians, the very act of creation and the love of God in Christ for all creation, stands as a constant reminder that, while we humans are special, we are also just a part of God's story of creation. To quote again from the World Council of Churches, from the report of the 1991 General Assembly on the theme Come Holy Spirit – Renew the Whole Creation:

> The divine presence of the Spirit in creation binds us human beings together with all created life. We are accountable before God in and to the community of life, an accountability which has been imagined in various ways: as servants, stewards and trustees, as tillers and keepers, as priests of creation, as nurturers, as co-creators. This requires attitudes of compassion and humility, respect and reverence.

For some Christians, the way forward lies in a rediscovery of distinctive teachings, lifestyles and insights contained within their tradition. For others, it requires a radical rethinking of what it means to be Christian. For yet others, there is still a struggle to reconcile centuries of human-centred Christian teaching with the truths which the environmentalists are telling us about the state of the world we are responsible for creating. For all of them, the core remains the belief in the Creator God who so loved the world that he sent his only begotten Son, that whoever believes in him should have eternal life (John 3:16). In the past, we can now see, this promise of life eternal has often been interpreted by the churches as meaning only human life. The challenge to all Christians is to discover anew the truth that God's love and liberation is for all creation, not just humanity; to realise that we should have been stewards, priests, co-creators with God for the rest of creation but have actually often been the ones responsible for its destruction; and to seek new ways of living and being Christians which will restore that balance and give the hope of life to so much of the endangered planet.

This statement was compiled and endorsed by the
Ecumenical Patriarchate of Constantinople,
the World Council of Churches and the
Vatican Franciscan Centre of Environmental Studies.

HINDUISM
after Swami Vibudhesha Teertha

'I call you brothers and sisters because we all
Worship one God – please believe it', you say

And how else could we believe all we believe
If it wasn't for this one thing pervading everything ?

But already you're off, small as you are
Showing us the sheer scale of it
                                        as your hands wave

And your voice breaks, screeches gleefully free
As you turn your treatise into a Sound Poem
So we have to turn the volume down

No microphone needed ! Your *agni*, exclaiming
'This is the Lord', this earth, this place
And 'earth is a dear, dear daughter of the sun'
As the spaces between stars weave in your throat –

And 'you have to love Her, to be attached to Her
You have to learn how to love her to keep her happy'
And do you ? Can we bear such simplicity ?

'God dwells in every heart of All His Children'
'The Lord has many children – many, many prophets',
And that could be each of us here as you smile

Almost shyly, your sari coming loose around your shoulders
Revealing your open chest and wooden strung beads
Because you know, as we smile
That only the heart can free the heart
That there is only one language that is feeling
We have to let go, like this, to feel –

That 'spiritual happiness is the sweetest happiness'
And that the price of one jetplane could feed thousands

Here on the living heart's ground.

Jay Ramsay

HINDUISM
Basic Hindu Environmental Teachings:

SUSTAINING THE BALANCE
Swami Vibudhesha Teertha

THESE DAYS it looks as if human beings have forgotten that a particular natural condition on Earth enabled life to come into existence and evolve to the human level. Humanity is disturbing this natural condition on which his existence, along with the existence of all other forms of life, depends. This is like the action of a wood-cutter cutting a tree at the trunk, on the branch on which he is sitting. According to Hindu religion, 'dharanath dharma ucyate' – that which sustains all species of life and helps to maintain harmonious relationship among them is *dharma* – and that which disturbs such ecology is adharma.

Hindu religion wants its followers to live a simple life. It does not allow people to go on increasing their material wants. People are meant to learn to enjoy spiritual happiness, so that to derive a sense of satisfaction and fulfilment, they need not run after material pleasures and disturb nature's checks and balances. They have to milk a cow and enjoy; not cut at the udder of the cow with greed to enjoy what is not available in the natural course. Do not use anything belonging to nature, such as oil, coal or forest, at a greater rate than you can replenish it. For example, do not destroy birds, fish, earthworms and even bacteria which play vital ecological roles – once they are annihilated you cannot recreate them. Thus only can you avoid becoming bankrupt and the life cycle can continue for a long, long time.

'Conserve ecology or perish' is the message of the *Bhagavad Gita* – a dialogue between Sri Krishna and Arjuna which is a clear and precise Life Science. It is narrated in the third chapter of this great work that a life without contribution towards the preservation of ecology is a life of sin and a life without specific purpose or use. The ecological cycle is explained in verses 3.14–16:

All living bodies subsist on food grains, which are produced from rains. Rains are produced from performance of *yajna* [sacrifice], and *yajna* is born of prescribed duties. Regulated activities are prescribed in the Vedas, and the Vedas are directly manifested from the Supreme Personality of Godhead. Consequently the all-pervading Transcendence is eternally situated in acts of sacrifice. My dear Arjuna, one who does not follow in human life the cycle of sacrifice thus established by the Vedas certainly lives a life full of sin. Living only for the satisfaction of the senses, such a person lives in vain.

Life is sustained by different kinds of food; rainfall produces food; timely movement of clouds brings rains; to get the clouds moving on time *yajna*, religious sacrifice, helps; *yajna* is performed through rituals; those actions which produce rituals belong only to God; God is revealed by the Vedas; the Vedas are preserved by the human mind; and the human mind is nourished by food. This is the cycle which helps the existence of all forms of life on this globe. One who does not contribute to the maintenance of this cycle is considered as a destroyer of all life here. When the Lord desired to create life, He created the Sun, Moon and Earth, and through them a congenial atmosphere for life to come into being. Therefore the Sun, Moon, Earth, Stars and all objects in the universe jointly, not individually, create the atmosphere for the creation, sustenance or destruction of everything in the universe. The Earth is the only daughter of the Sun to produce children. The Moon is essential for the creation of the right atmosphere for those children to exist and evolve. This we say because of the influence of the Moon on high and low tides in our rivers and oceans. This is narrated also in the *Bhagavad Gita*:

I become the moon and thereby supply the juice of life to all vegetables.

We cannot refute this influence of the Moon on life. It is proved by the movement of all liquid on this globe depending on the movement of the Moon. Therefore ecology in totality must be preserved: just a part of it would not suffice.

Hinduism is a religion which is very near to nature. It asks its followers to see God in every object in the Universe. Worship of God in air, water, fire, Sun, Moon, Stars and Earth is specially recommended. Earth is worshipped as the spouse of God. Hence very dear and near to God. All lives on Earth are considered as children of God and Earth.

Sri Krishna in the *Bhagavad Gita* says,

I am pervading the Universe. All objects in the Universe rest on me as pearls on the thread of a garland.

The *Upanishads* narrate that after creating the Universe, the creator entered into each and every object to help them maintain their inter-relationship. The *Upanishad* says 'tat sristva ta devanu pravisat': after creating the universe He entered into every object created. Therefore to contribute towards the maintenance of this inter-relationship becomes worship of God. Hindus believe that there is soul in all plants and animals. One has to do penance even for killing plants and animals for food. This daily penance is called *visva deva*. *Visva deva* is nothing but an offering of prepared food to the Creator, asking His pardon.

The Hindu religion gives great importance to protecting cattle. At every Hindu house there is a cow and it is worshipped. The cow is a great friend of humans. It nourishes us through its milk and provides manure to grow our food. This it does without any extra demand – it lives on the fodder got while growing our food. Advanced countries have started to realise the harmful effects of consuming food grown with chemical manure. When we use chemical manure, the top soil loses its fertility. This generation has no right to use up all the fertility of the soil and leave behind an unproductive land for future generations.

There is no life which is inferior. All lives enjoy the same importance in the Universe and all play their fixed roles. They are to function together and no link in the chain is to be lost. If some link is lost, the whole ecological balance would be disturbed. All kinds of life – insects, birds and animals – contribute towards the maintenance of ecological balance, but what is man's contribution towards this? He is an intelligent animal, therefore his contribution should be the biggest. But we find the absence of his contribution. On the other hand he is nullifying the benefits of the contributions made by other species of life. He is disturbing the balance because of his greed for material enjoyment and his craze for power. He does not allow earthworms and bacteria to maintain the fertility of the soil by using chemical manures and insecticides which kill them. He destroys plants and forests indiscriminately and comes in the way of plants providing oxygen essential for the very existence of life. By destroying plants and forests he becomes an agent for increasing the deadly carbon dioxide in the atmosphere. He pollutes the air by burning oil for all sorts of machines. He produces unhealthy sounds through his various machineries and instruments which cause sound pollution. By building towns and cities in the banks of rivers he pollutes all water in rivers. The Hindu religion holds all rivers as holy; polluting them is a big sin. It encourages the planting of trees like Tulasi, Neem, Peepal and the like which are rich in medicinal properties.

Rishis gave the navel to Brahma, the creator, and to the sustainer Vishnu they gave the heart as His abode. The destroyer, Shiva, is given control of the brain. By doing this they wanted us to know that the language of the heart only can sustain us – when we start speaking through the language of the mind our destruction becomes inevitable. Therefore, a thinking animal has to be very careful while it uses its mental abilities: these are to be applied only with spiritual background. Mind is to act as our friend and not as our enemy. It is to function under our control – we should not succumb to its control. 'Mana eva manusyanam karanam bandha moksayoh': for man, mind is the cause of bondage and mind is the cause of liberation (*Amrita Bindhu Upanishad* 2).

There should be a purpose for the creation of man. What it might be! Man could be the sustainer of inter-relationship among numerous life species on Earth. He is one who can see God, and all objects, as the controller and sustainer of ecological balance. All other animals play their roles without knowing what they are doing, but man does everything with full consciousness. God created man's mind to see His own reflection as in a mirror. Man's mind can meditate on God and know him more and more. When he develops consciousness of the presence of God and His continuous showering of blessings on the universe, man develops deep love for Him. To enjoy this nectar of love, God created man. Only man has time-space conception. Therefore, he only can see God, pervading time-space, conserving the ecological balance which is the greatest boon bestowed on the universe by God. Though he can not contribute towards the conservation in the same way as other animals do man can help all lives and other objects in the universe to play their roles effectively by persuading God through prayers of love to grant them the required energy and directions. 'Yavat bhumandalam datte samrigavana karnanam, tavat tisthati medhinyam santatih putra pautriki': so long as the Earth preserves her forests and wildlife, man's progeny will continue to exist. This is the Hindu approach towards the conservation of ecology.

SACRIFICE AND PROTECTION
Dr Sheshagiri Rao

Sacrifice

> The Creator, in the beginning, created men together with sacrifice, and said, 'By this you shall multiply. Let this be your cow of plenty and give you the milk of your desires. With sacrifice you will nourish the gods, and the gods will nourish you. Thus you will obtain the Highest Good. (*Bhagavad Gita* 3,10–11)

Sacrifice does not just mean ritual worship – it means an act which protects life. Personal health depends on eyes, ears and other sense organs working together in harmony; human prosperity and happiness depend on a well-ordered society and nature; the universe is sustained by the cosmic powers such as the sun and moon working together in unison. Sacrifice reinvigorates the powers that sustain the world by securing cosmic stability and social order. It activates the positive forces of the universe, and protects the Earth from degeneration.

Non-violence

God's creation is sacred. Humanity does not have the right to destroy what it cannot create. Humans have to realise the interconnectedness of living entities and emphasise the idea of moral responsibility to oneself, one's society and the world as a whole. In our cosmic journey, we are involved in countless cycles of births and deaths. Life progresses into higher forms or regresses into lower forms of life based upon our good or bad *karma*. Kinship exists between all forms of life. Reincarnation warns us against treating lower forms of life with cruelty.

Cow protection

Man has evolved from lower forms of life. He is, therefore, related to the whole creation. The principle of cow protection symbolises human responsibility to the sub-human world. It also indicates reverence for all forms of life. The cow serves humans throughout its life, and even after death. The milk of the cow runs in our blood. Its contributions to the welfare of the family and the community are countless. Hindus pray daily for the welfare of cows. When the cows are cared for, the world at all levels will find happiness and peace.

Earth as mother

Hindus revere the Earth as mother. She feeds, shelters and clothes us. Without her we cannot survive. If we as children do not take care of her we diminish her ability to take care of us. Unfortunately the Earth herself is now being undermined by our scientific and industrial achievements.

BREAKING THE FAMILY
SHRIVATSA GOSWAMI

> Let there be peace in the heavens, the Earth, the atmosphere, the water, the herbs, the vegetation, among the divine beings and in Brahman, the absolute reality. Let everything be at peace and in peace. Only then will we find peace.

According to Hindu philosophy, the goal of human life is the realisation of the state of peace. *Dharma*, loosely translated as religion, is the source by which peace can be fully realised. This peace is not the stillness of death; it is a dynamic harmony among all the diverse facets of life. Humanity, as part of the natural world, can contribute through *dharma* to this natural harmony.

The natural harmony which should exist in the play of energies between humanity and the natural world is now disrupted by the weakest player in the game – humanity. Although it is the totality of this game that provides our nourishment, through ignorance of our own natural limits we destroy this source of nourishment.

This awareness of ecological play or playful ecology is inseparable from awareness of the need for friendship and play as the real basis for human relationship. The family within which these relationships are nourished is not limited to its human members. Just as the human child has to be nourished by

Mother Nature, and the human spirit has to be embraced and loved by beautiful nature, so the human being who has grown old or sick has to be supported by caring nature. If humans distress the mother, rape the beauty and beat the caring nurse, what happens? The relationship collapses, and the family is broken.

The Sanskrit for family is *parivara*, and environment is *paryavarana*. If we think of the environment as our home and all of its members as our family it is clear that the key to conserving nature is devotion, love – giving and serving. Nature, *prakriti*, as the feminine can give and serve. But the role of humanity, *purusha*, is then to protect. Nowadays *purusha*, humanity, is interested not in protecting but in exploiting, so *prakriti*, nature, has to defend herself. This is why we see nature in her furious manifestation – in drought, floods or hurricanes. If we rape the mother's womb she has convulsions, and we blame her for devastating earthquakes. If we denude her of her lush hair and beautiful skin, she punishes us by withholding food and water.

As it is through ignorance that we destroy our relationships in the family and within the environment, that ignorance becomes the root cause of our suffering. The best way to get rid of this ignorance is to unlearn what is wrong. This unlearning is shaped not only in the school but in the family and community, and it has to begin with the very young.

Traditional Hindu education covers all facets of life – economic, political, cultural and above all religious. Whether we speak of Krishna, of Chaitanya, or of Gandhi, we see that they drew no clear division between the economic or political and the religious or cultural facets of life. The body and mind are in the service of the heart. In the same way politics and economics are rooted in and guided by religion and culture, and ultimately by spiritual experience.

This statement was based on papers and comments submitted by:

DR SHESHAGIRI RAO
Chief Editor of *Encyclopedia of Hinduism*

SWAMI CHIDANANDA SARASVATI
Founder of *India Heritage Research Foundation*
Spiritual Head of Parmarth Niketan Ashram.

SHRIVATSA GOSWAMI
Vaishnava Acharya of Shri Radharaman Temple, Vrindavan
Chairman of the Vrindavan Conservation Project

SWAMI VIBUDHESHA TEERTHA
Acharya of Madhvacarya Vaishnavas, Udupi
Central Advisory Committee Member of the Visva Hindu Parishad

Compiled and edited by RANCHOR PRIME of ICOREC
Consultants to the Organising Committee for the Summit on Religions and Conservation.

ISLAM

after Prof. Muhammed Hyder

Your God Of the Absolute
In His searching blazing desert light
Is nowhere to be found over your head:
Your presence is here, and your warmth is deep,
And as broad as your shoulders in its embrace:

Soul, we called it, remember?
In your patient ear like a mountain
And in the slow rooted movement of your speech

But let's be practical: you number the trees
Replanted with drip irrigation –
You talk of cleaning water, and organic farming,
As you ask 'How can we reach the millions worldwide?'

And let's be real: what blocks out the light?
Those with their axes to grind – and those that deny
That 'daily bread doesn't exist for most of these people'
As we sit, well-fed, in this tasteful library
Not one of us starving, or only of heart –

And that is the truth beyond our minds
Old Grandfather Adam, as you spell it:
This Oneness, this Allah is all over the ground
Calling our names out loud.

Jay Ramsay

ISLAM

MAN'S MOST primordial concepts of religion relate to the environment. Man's history on planet Earth is, in a geological scale, very short indeed. Planet Earth itself is a mere 3,800 million years old. Man only appeared one or maybe two million years ago. Most of the physical patterns of planet Earth were probably in place – broadly speaking – by the time Man evolved. Apart from what he first saw, he also probably witnessed some spectacular changes himself. He must, at the very least, have gone through one Ice Age and seen some graphic volcanic eruptions – assuming he was able to avoid its consequences. The environment, therefore, very probably induced the first thoughts of a Super-Being – a God, if you like – whose manifestations lay in Man's immediate surroundings.

Man's environment also provided another dimension in his relationship with Nature. To survive in a given environment, Man had to adjust what he takes from that environment to what can give him sustainable yields on (at the very least) an annual basis. In effect this meant that early Man had to learn to conserve at an early age. Being largely dependent on what was available rather than from what he could cultivate, he entered into a partnership with the environment. To take more than the regenerative capacity of the environment could lead to serious subsequent exhaustion – quite rightly seen as harsh retribution from an angry God. The converse situation of exploitation with moderation led to sustained yields which were (again, quite rightly) taken as having pleased God.

This relationship between conservation and religion is thus not only a natural one but also probably as old as the proverbial hills. But when we quickly open most of the pages of Man's history on planet Earth and come to last three hundred years or so, we find the advent of the Industrial Revolution. The Industrial Revolution made possible the production of large quantities of goods in a very short time. That meant that raw materials in ever-increasing quantities had to be found to feed the hungry mills ready to convert them into finished or semi-finished goods. The consequences of the Industrial Revolution were many

– economic, social and environmental. The material achievements of the human race in the past one hundred or so years have overshadowed the contributions made by all past civilisations. The Industrial Revolution that took place in Europe in the 18th and 19th centuries exacted a high social and environmental cost. Now these costs are even higher and more universal, being manifestly so in the great urban centres of the world. The paradox of 'progress' today is the easily perceived correlation between complex consumer societies and the degeneration of the human being. Or as John Seymour puts it:

> We see men now wherever we look, so blinded by arrogance and the worship of man as God that they are doing things no one but the insane would do... men maddened by the belief that they are both omniscient and omnipotent, that they are indeed, God.

The Industrial Revolution also proclaimed a new revival of another God – Mammon. Mammon regrettably has no respect for environmental integrity – nor do his followers. The last 250 years have seen a growing decimation of ever more pristine areas of Nature to feed the insatiable industrial cuckoo and its resultant consumerism. Forests – particularly tropical forests – have been systematically hewn down, the seas ransacked, the lands made totally dependent on a host of inorganic fertilizers and pesticides for food production, wastes galore have filled the seas, the rivers and the lakes not to mention the land fills.

We must also take note that the 'unmatched material progress' of this century we are often fond of talking about has only been possible for the few: that is the population of the northern hemisphere and a small minority among the peoples of the south. This is usually translated as less than 25 per cent of the world's population consuming over 75 per cent of the world's resources. This rate of consumption by a minority of the human species has caused unparalleled climatic change, eco-system disintegration and species extinction, and as a report by WWF (World Wide Fund For Nature) observes:

> loss of bio-diversity worldwide, and the combination of global warming with other human pressures will present the greatest challenge in conservation for decades to come.

This would lead us to conclude that there is a profound and inherent contradiction in the efforts made by the 'North' to keep ahead of the rest as consumers, and the push by the remaining 75 per cent of the world's population to catch up. Given this scenario, if just Eastern Europe or Russia or India or China, managed to raise their standards of living by just a few percentage points, then the consequences of putting this extra load on the earth's eco-system, which is already under severe strain, would be catastrophic.

This is the background against which the followers of the relatively ancient, environmentally conscious (indeed environmentally concerned) God have gathered to re-examine and to restate their own commitment to environmental integrity from their own individual religion's standpoint. We for our part will look at the underpinnings of conservation in Islam.

Islam and Conservation

There are several Islamic principles which, when taken individually, seem to have little bearing on conservation. Together, however, they add up to a clear concept of the Islamic view on conservation. We shall now annotate these principles briefly.

Tawheed

The first Islamic principle which relates to conservation is that of the Oneness of Allah, or *Tawheed*. This principle is absolutely fundamental to Islam. Every Muslim must believe in this Oneness of Allah. It is said by some *Ulamaa* that some two-thirds of Prophet Muhammad's (SAW) early preaching – and indeed of the Qur'an itself – were and are dedicated purely to endorsing this very Oneness of Allah. One indivisible God means to a Muslim that there is no separate deity for each of the many attributes that to Muslims belong to the One Universal God who is also God of the Universe.

Tawheed is the monotheistic principle of Islam and it begins by declaring that 'there is no God but God' (the second half of this declaration asserts that 'Muhammad is His Messenger'). We are for the present concerned with the first part which affirms that there is nothing other than the Absolute, the Eternal, All Powerful Creator. This is the bedrock statement of the Oneness of the Creator from which stems everything else.

> It is the primordial testimony of the unity of all creation and the interlocking grid of the natural order of which man is intrinsically a part. (*Islam, Ecology and the World Order*)

God says in the Qur'an:

> 112.001. Say: He is Allah the One and Only;
>
> 112.002. Allah the Eternal Absolute;
>
> 112.003. He begetteth not nor is He begotten;
>
> 112.004. And there is none like unto Him.

God is Real; not an abstract idea or concept; He is One, the Everlasting Refuge for all creation.

Man's relation to God

The emphasis on *Tawheed* is significant unto itself but it is even more relevant to the present discussion by virtue of defining a Muslim's relationship to Allah. The Omniscience and Omnipotence of Allah means, by definition, that a Muslim's relationship to Allah is total. To Him – and to Him only – should Man refer for all his needs: physical, mental and spiritual. Indeed, Allah would not have it any other way. As He says in the Qur'an:

> 004.048. Allah forgiveth not that partners should be set up with him; but He forgiveth anything else to whom He pleaseth; to set up partners with Allah is to devise a sin most heinous indeed.

But Allah is not only the One Indivisible God. He is also the Universal God as well as the Lord of the Universe:

> 001.002. Praise be to Allah, Lord of the Worlds

And again:

> 006.071. Say: 'Allah's guidance is the (only) guidance and we have been directed to submit ourselves to the Lord of the worlds'.

> 006.072. To establish regular prayers and to fear Allah; for it is to Him that we shall be gathered together.

> 006.073. It is He Who created the heavens and the earth in true (proportions): the day He saith 'Be' Behold! it is. His Word is the truth. His will be the dominion the day the trumpet will be blown. He knoweth the Unseen as well as that which is open. For He is the Wise well acquainted (with all things).

To Allah belongs the Earth and the Heavens

Yet another principle which underpins Islamic commitment to the conservation of nature and natural resources is the principle of divine ownership of all that exists on earth and in the heavens – animate and inanimate. There are countless verses in the Holy Qur'an which state this. A few are given below.

In the celebrated Ayatul Kursiyy:

> 002.255. Allah! there is no Allah but He the living the Self-subsisting Eternal. No slumber can seize him nor sleep. His are all things in the heavens and on earth. Who is there can intercede in His presence except as He permitteth? He knoweth what (appeareth to his creatures as) before or after or behind them. Nor shall they compass aught of his knowledge except as He willeth. His throne doth extend over the heavens and the earth and He feeleth no fatigue in guarding and preserving them. For He is the Most High the Supreme (in glory).

And again:

> 004.171. To Him belong all things in the heavens and on earth. And enough is Allah as a Disposer of affairs.

> 006.013. To Him belongeth all that dwelleth (or lurketh) in the night and the day. For He is the One Who heareth and knoweth all things.

> 020.006. To Him belongs what is in the heavens and on earth and all between them and all beneath the soil.

> 021.019. To Him belong all (creatures) in the heavens and on earth: even those who are in His (very) Presence are not too proud to serve Him nor are they (ever) weary (of His service):

But we are reminded that all things animate and inanimate, in their own ways, submit themselves to the Glory of Allah. There are many verses in the Qur'an about this:

> 030.026. To Him belongs every being that is in the heavens and on earth: all are devoutly obedient to Him.

And again:

> 062.001. Whatever is in the heavens and on earth doth declare the Praises and Glory of Allah the Sovereign the Holy One the Exalted in Might the Wise.

Thus Allah, the One Indivisible God, the Universal God and the Lord of the Universe is the Owner also of all that is in the universe, including Man. After all, we are reminded to say constantly:

> 002.155. Be sure We shall test you with something of fear and hunger some loss in goods or lives or the fruits (of your toil) but give glad tidings to those who patiently persevere.

> 002.156. Who say when afflicted with calamity: 'To Allah we belong and to Him is our return'.

The above set of principles – all taken from Islam's ultimate authority, the Holy Qu'ran – set the perspectives of the relationship of Man to God and of God to the environment in its totality. A second set of principles that the Holy Qur'an enunciates prescribe Man's relationship to the environment after, of course, Man has accepted the preceding principles.

Man and the Khalifa

The most important of this second set of principles is that which defines man's role and his responsibilities in the natural order that Allah provided. The appointment of Man as a *Khalifa*, or the role of guardian, is the sacred duty God has given to the human race. The appointment of Man to this elevated position gives rise to the one occasion when the Angels actually questioned Allah's decision as seen in the following verses:

> 002.030. Behold thy Lord said to the angels: 'I will create a viceregent on earth.' They said 'Wilt thou place therein one who will make mischief therein and shed blood? Whilst we do celebrate Thy praises and glorify Thy holy (name)?' He said: 'I know what ye know not.'

> 002.031. And He taught Adam the nature of all things; then He placed them before the angels and said: 'Tell Me the nature of these if ye are right.'

> 002.032. They said: 'Glory to Thee of knowledge we have none save that Thou hast taught us: in truth it is Thou who art perfect in knowledge and wisdom.'

> 002.033. He said: 'O Adam! tell them their natures.' When he had told them Allah said: 'Did I not tell you that I know the secrets of heaven and earth and I know what ye reveal and what ye conceal?'

> 002.034. And behold We said to the angels: 'Bow down to Adam'; and they bowed down, not so Iblis he refused and was haughty he was of those who reject Faith.

Clearly Allah preferred unprogrammed freewill of Man to the pre-programmed goodness of Angels!

And again:

> 006.165. It is He who hath made you (His) agents inheritors of the earth: He hath raised you in ranks some above others: that he may try you in the gifts He hath given you: for thy Lord is quick in punishment: yet He is indeed Oft-Forgiving Most Merciful. '

The exercise of the viceregency is defined in the Qur'an by another set of principles between which Man's privileges as well as his responsibilities are clearly defined. We shall deal with these briefly in the following paragraphs.

Mizaan

One of the most important attributes conferred on Man is the faculty of reasoning. This, above all, might well be the deciding fact or in his appointment as God's viceregent on Earth. The relevant verses reminding Man of this faculty are below:

> 055.001. (Allah) Most Gracious!

> 055.002. It is He Who has taught the Qur'an.

> 055.003. He has created man:

> 055.004. He has taught him speech (and Intelligence)

> 055.005. The sun and the moon follow courses (exactly) computed;

> 055.006. And the herbs and the trees – both (alike) bow in adoration.

> 055.007. And the firmament has He raised high and He has set up the balance (of Justice)

> 055.008. In order that ye may not transgress (due) balance.

> 055.009. So establish weight with justice and fall not short in the balance.

> 055.010. It is He Who has spread out the earth for (His) creatures:

> 055.011. Therein is fruit and date-palms producing spathes (enclosing dates):

> 055.012. Also corn with (its) leaves and stalk for fodder and sweet-smelling plants.

> 055.013. Then which of the favours of your Lord will ye deny?

Man was not created to function exclusively on instinct. The 'explanation' was taught to him because he had the capacity to reason and understand. There is order and purpose in the whole pattern of creation. The Sun and Moon following stable orbits make life possible. The whole universe is in submission to the Creator – the stars that enable us to steer courses and the trees that give us sustenance, shelter and other uses. The world functions only because creation follows a pre-ordained pattern. Man then has a responsibility by virtue of being able to reason, to behave justly, 'to transgress not in the balance'. We owe this to ourselves as much as for the rest of creation.

Justice

The capacity to reason and to balance intellectual judgment would in itself be insufficient without the additional moral commitment to Justice. And this is what the Qur'an prescribes for Muslims:

> 004.135. O ye who believe! stand out firmly for justice as witnesses to Allah even as against yourselves or your parents or your kin and whether it be (against) rich or poor: for Allah can best protect both. Follow not the lusts (of your hearts) lest ye swerve and if ye distort (justice) or decline to do justice verily Allah is well-acquainted with all that ye do.

And again:

> 004.085. Whoever recommends and helps a good cause becomes a partner therein: and whoever recommends and helps an evil cause shares in its burden: and Allah hath power over all things.

> 004.058. Allah doth command you to render back your trusts to those to whom they are due; and when ye judge between man and man that ye judge with justice: verily how excellent is the teaching which He giveth you! for Allah is He who heareth and seeth all things.

And again:

> 005.009. O ye who believe! stand out firmly for Allah as witnesses to fair dealing and let not the hatred of others to you make you swerve to wrong and depart from justice. Be just: that is next to Piety: and fear Allah for Allah is well-acquainted with all that ye do.

> 005.045. (They are fond of) listening to falsehood of devouring anything forbidden. If they do come to thee either judge between them or decline to interfere. If thou decline they cannot hurt thee in the least. If thou judge judge in equity between them; for Allah loveth those who judge in equity.

Use but do not abuse

Several times in the Qur'an, Man is invited to make use of the nourishing goods that Allah has placed on earth for him, but abuse – particularly through extravagance and excess – is strictly forbidden. Sometimes this is stated in one breath, so to speak. Sometimes they are stated separately. But the message is the same as the following verse indicates:

> 007.031. O children of Adam!... eat and drink: but waste not by excess for Allah loveth not the wasters.

There are as many invitations to partake of Nature as provided for Man and for other creatures of the Earth as there are for the avoidance of wasteful extravagance. Time and again, Allah reminds us that He loveth not wasters.

> 006.141. It is He who produceth gardens with trellises and without and dates and tilth with produce of all kinds and olives and pomegranates similar (in kind) and different (in variety): eat of their fruit in their season but render the dues that are proper on the day that the harvest is gathered. But waste not by excess: for Allah loveth not the wasters.

Fitra

The last principle which we bring forth in our examination of the Qur'anic underpinnings of conservation is that of *fitra*. *Fitra* can be taken as perhaps the most direct injunction by Allah to Man to conserve the environment and not to change the balance of His creation. This is specifically contained in the verse below:

> 030.030. So set thou thy face steadily and truly to the Faith: (Establish) Allah's handiwork according to the pattern on which He has made mankind: no change (let there be) in the work (wrought) by Allah: that is the standard Religion: but most among mankind understand not.

Thus, Islam teaches that humanity is an integral part of the environment, it is part of the creation of Almighty God. We remain deeply locked into the natural domain despite the fact that there is talk of bringing the environment to the people as though we are independent of it.

The power given to man by God is seen in Islam to be limited by the responsibilities he bears, not only towards God and other men and women, but also towards the rest of creation.

Seyyed Hossein Nasr says:

> The Divine Law (*al shariah*) is explicit in extending the religious duties of man to the natural order and the environment. (*The Need for a Sacred Science*)

The Conclusion

As we indicated at the beginning, there are a number of Qur'anic principles which, taken separately, do not have an obvious connection with conservation. But taken in their totality, they state in clear terms that Allah, the One True God is the Universal God and the Creator of the Universe and indeed, the Owner of the Universe. To Him belong all the animate and inanimate objects, all of whom should or do submit themselves to Him. Allah, in His Wisdom, appointed Man, the creature that He has conferred with the faculty of Reason and with Freewill, to be His viceregent on Earth. And while Allah has invited Man to partake of the fruits of the Earth for his rightful nourishment and enjoyment, He has also directed Man not to waste that which Allah has provided for him – for He loveth not wasters. Furthermore, Allah has also ordered Man to administer his responsibilities with Justice. Above all, Man should conserve the balance of

Allah's creation on Earth. By virtue of his intelligence, Man (when he believes in the One Universal Allah, the Creator of the Universe), is the only creation of Allah to be entrusted with the overall responsibility of maintaining planet Earth in the overall balanced ecology that Man found. If biologists believe that Man is the greatest agent of ecological change on the surface of the Earth, is it not Man who, drawn from the brink, will – for his own good – abandon Mammon and listen to the prescriptions of God on the conservation of his environment and the environment of all the creatures on Earth? The Islamic answer to this question is decisively in the affirmative.

This statement compiled by:
Mohamed Hyder
Ihsan Mahasneh

REFERENCES

The numbers at the beginning of each Qur'anic quotation refer to the chapter and verse(s) of the Qur'an. The translation used is by ABDALLA YUSUF ALI.

SEYYED HOSSEIN NASR, *The Need for a Sacred Science*, Curzon Press, England, 1993

SEYYED HOSSEIN NASR, *Man and Nature*, Mandala/Unwin, London, 1990

FAZLUN KHALID, *Islam, Ecology and the World Order*, a paper delivered at a conference on Islam and the Environment, UK, 1993

JAINISM
after Dr L.M. Singhvi

You speak of a telescopic sense of urgency
By focusing now on what matters:

We have looked through the wrong end of the lens for too long,
And we need to turn it down from the sky

And what do we see? Every blade of grass,
Every flower, and every littered piece of waste...
'Sacred and secular' as you say
'God created *one* world', and this is it

There is nowhere else to escape.

And when you speak like this, you speak
'Not as a Jain, or a Hindu or a Buddhist, but a human being'
Nor as a High Commissioner, but as yourself –

No rhetoric now –
And the garden of goodwill you speak of is real
It has a time, a place, and an extent*

And as you say it
'I cannot resolve the theological problems
I am too small, I am too humble
I must get on here and now...'

As you gaze the right way through the lens, and down.

* in Brent, East London

Jay Ramsay

JAINISM

JAINISM IS ONE of the oldest living religions. The term Jain means 'the follower of the Jinas' (spiritual victors), human teachers who attained omniscience. These teachers are also called *Tirthankaras* (ford-makers), those who help others escape the cycle of birth and death.

The twenty-fourth *Tirthankara*, called Mahavira, was born in 599 BC. At the age of thirty, he left home on a spiritual quest. After twelve years of trials and austerities, he attained omniscience. Eleven men became his *ganadharas*, chief disciples. At seventy-two Mahavira died and attained nirvana, that blissful state beyond life and death. Mahavira was not the founder of a new religion. He consolidated the faith by drawing together the teachings of the previous *Tirthankaras*, particularly those of his immediate predecessor, Parsva, who lived about 250 years earlier at Varnasi.

Initially the followers of Jainism lived throughout the Ganges Valley in India. Around 250 BC, most Jains migrated to the city of Mathura on the Yamuna River. Later, many travelled west to Rajasthan and Gujarat and south to Maharashtra and Karnataka where Jainism rapidly grew in popularity. The Jain population throughout the world is less than ten million, of which about one hundred thousand have settled overseas in North America, United Kingdom, Kenya, Belgium, Singapore, Hong Kong and Japan.

Jain Practices

Jains believe that to attain the higher stages of personal development, lay people must adhere to the three jewels (*ratna-traya*) namely enlightened worldview, true knowledge, and conduct based on enlightened worldview and true knowledge. They must endeavor to fulfill the *anuvratas* (small vows). These vows are:

Ahimsa (non-violence)
This is the fundamental vow and runs through the Jain tradition like a golden thread. It involves avoidance of violence in any form through word or deed

not only to human beings but to all nature. It means reverence for life in every form including plants and animals. Jains practise the principle of compassion for all living beings (*Jiva-daya*) at every step in daily life. Jains are vegetarians.

Satya (truthfulness)
'Tirthankara Mahavira' said Sachham Bhagwam (Truth is God).

Asteya (not stealing)
This is the principle of not taking what belongs to another. It means avoidance of greed and exploitation.

Brahmacharya (chastity)
This means practising restraint and avoiding sexual promiscuity.

Aparigraha (non-materialism)
For lay Jains, this means limiting their acquisition of material goods and contributing one's wealth and time to humanitarian charities and philanthropic causes.

Jain Beliefs

Anekantavada (non-one-sidedness)
This philosophy states that no single perspective on any issue contains the whole truth. It emphasises the concept of universal interdependence and specifically recommends that one should take into account the viewpoints of other species, other communities and nations and other human beings.

Loka (the universe)
Space is infinite but only a finite portion is occupied by what is known as the universe. Everything within the universe, whether sentient (*jiva*) or insentient (*ajiva*) is eternal, although the forms that a thing may take are transient. Jains preach and practise the principle of the duty of every human being to promote universal well being (*sarva-mangalya*).

Jiva (soul)
All living beings have an individual soul (*jiva*) which occupies the body, a conglomerate of atoms. At the time of death, the soul leaves the body and immediately takes birth in another. Attaining nirvana and thereby terminating this cycle of birth and death is the goal of Jain practice.

Ajiva (non-soul)
Ajiva is everything in the universe that is insentient, including matter, the media of motion and rest, time and space.

Karma
Is understood as a form of subtle matter which adheres to the soul as a result
of its actions of body, speech and mind. This accumulated *karma* is the cause
of the soul's bondage in the cycle of birth and death.

Moksha or nirvana (eternal liberation through enlightenment)
The ultimate aim of life is to emancipate the soul from the cycle of birth and
death. This is done by exhausting all bound *karmas* and preventing further
accumulation. To achieve *moksha*, it is necessary to have enlightened worldview, knowledge and conduct.

Jainism is fundamentally a religion of ecology and has turned ecology into a
religion. It has enabled Jains to create an environment-friendly value system and
code of conduct. Because of the insistence on rationality in the Jain tradition,
Jains are always ready and willing to look positively and with enthusiasm upon
environmental causes. In India and abroad, they are in the forefront of bringing
greater awareness and putting into practice their cardinal principles on ecology.
Their programmes have been modest and mostly self-funded through volunteers.

This statement compiled by:
Dr L.M. Singhvi
on behalf of the Institute of Jainology

JUDAISM
after Rabbi Arthur Hertzberg

'Three Jews, three opinions' – you laugh
Out of your modesty, relaxing the tension,
As the gift of your humour warms the air

And then the joke's on you, as your glasses
Slip briefly off your nose –
As you turn to gravity, to what matters here

And in that brief nakedness of your eyes
Everything you say resonates as it needs to, now

'Animals were not created to serve Man,
Nothing in Creation was created to serve Man,
We must change…'

As the green herb of Genesis drifts back
As you talk of the root we have ravaged and plucked
In the forests of our lungs and our breathing –

'To create the land of milk and honey again
That the Bible so warmly promises …'
– oh song of songs, of flesh with flesh
And flower with grass and stone, as one,
Song Of Songs sung into the wound –

Into the rape of our desecration…and now?

As you say it, it's not looking above, below, or back
But forward, into the sacred sign
You trace between your mouth and your finger, raised

In a language so like Deaf and Dumb.

Jay Ramsay

JUDAISM
The Environment – Jewish Perspectives
PROFESSOR NAHUM RAKOVER

Consider the work of God; for who can make that straight, which man has made crooked?
(*Eccles.* 7:13)

When God created Adam, he showed him all the trees of the Garden of Eden and said to him: See my works, how lovely they are, how fine they are. All I have created, I created for you. Take care not to corrupt and destroy my universe, for if you destroy it, no one will come after you to put it right.'
(*Ecclesiastes Rabbah* 7)

THE PRESENT paper is concerned with the vast and complex problem of protecting our natural environment from pollution and destruction, so that we can live in God's world while enjoying its beauty and deriving from it the maximum physical and spiritual benefit.

In Jewish sources, the rationale for man's obligation to protect nature may be found in the biblical expression, 'For the earth is Mine' (*Lev.* 25:23). The Bible informs us that the earth is not subject to man's absolute ownership, but is rather given to man 'to use and protect' (*Gen.* 2:15).

From biblical sources which refer to man's 'dominion' over nature, it would appear as though man was granted unlimited control of his world, as we find in *Genesis* 1:26:

> And God said, 'Let us make man in our image, after our likeness; and let them have dominion over the fish of the sea, and over the fowl of the air, and over the cattle and over all the earth, and over every creeping thing that creeps upon the earth.'

And again in *Genesis* 1:28:

> And God blessed them [Adam and Eve...] 'Be fruitful, and multiply, and fill the earth and subdue it; and have dominion over the fish of the sea, and over the fowl of the air, and over every living thing that creeps upon the earth.'

Rav Kook[1] has an insightful understanding of the idea:[2]

> There can be no doubt to any enlightened or thoughtful person, that the 'domin-ion' mentioned in the Bible in the phrase, 'and have dominion over the fish of the sea, and over the fowl of the air, and over every living thing that creeps upon the earth,' is not the dominion of a tyrant who deals harshly with his people and servants in order to achieve his own personal desires and whims. It would be unthinkable to legislate so repugnant a subjugation and have it forever engraved upon the world of God, who is good to all and whose mercy extends to all He has created, as is written, 'the earth is founded upon mercy'. (*Ps* 89:3).

Three Things which Grant Man Tranquillity

The Sages of the *Talmud* gave expression to the environment's effect on man's spirit in their statement.[3]

> Three things restore a man's consciousness: [beautiful] sounds, sights, and smells. Three things enlarge a man's spirit: a beautiful dwelling, a beautiful wife, and beautiful clothes.

Life in the City

The Sages of the *Talmud* also noted that the environment undergoes more dam-age in large cities than in small towns. In explaining a law of the *Mishnah*[4] that a spouse may not compel his mate to move from a village to a large city, the *Talmud* cites the reasoning of R Yosi ben Hanina,[5] 'Life is more difficult in the city.' Rashi explains:[6]

> Because so many live there, and they crowd their houses together, and there is no air, whereas in villages there are gardens and orchards close to the homes, and the air is good.[7]

One Who Threw Stones into the Public Domain

We learn of the obligation of the individual to protect the public domain from a story brought in the *Tosefta*:[8]

> It happened that a certain person was removing stones from his ground onto public ground when a pious man found him and said, 'Fool, why do you remove stones from ground which is not yours to ground which is yours?' The man laughed at him. Some time later he had was compelled to sell his field, and when he was walking on that public ground, he stumbled over the stones he had thrown there. He then said, 'How well did that pious man say to me, Why do you remove stones from ground which is not yours to ground which is yours?'

In other words, the terms 'public domain' and 'private domain' are not necessar-ily identical to the concepts 'mine' and 'not mine'. What was once my private domain might one day not be mine, while the public domain will always remain my domain.

Protection of the Environment and the Love of Man

In addition to the rules governing man's relations with his fellow man, which are based upon the biblical imperative, 'Love your neighbour as yourself' (*Lev.* 19:18), norms were established for man's treatment of plants, animals[9] and even the inanimate elements of nature.

When approaching the subject of environmental protection, we must be careful to maintain the proper balance between protection of the environment and protection of man. The proper balance in this context is certainly not one of equality between man and nature. The relationship between man and nature is one of ownership – albeit limited. In our enthusiasm for protecting the environment, we must not forget man's interests or his role in the scheme of creation. Love of nature may not take precedence over love of man. We must avoid at all costs the error of those who were known as lovers of animals yet perpetrated the worst crimes imaginable against their fellow men.

The proper balance must also be maintained between individual interests and the interest of the public. Sometimes an individual's act may harm the community, as when a person builds a factory that pollutes the environment with industrial waste. Sometimes, however, it is the community that is interested in a factory although it constitutes a serious infringement upon an individual's ability to enjoy his own home and surroundings.

When discussing the quality of the environment, we must remember that the environment also comprises the persons living in it – individuals and community. Protection of the environment, by itself, cannot solve conflicts of interest, though it can extend the range of factors considered when seeking solutions to problems. Solutions must, in the final analysis, be based upon economic, social, and moral considerations.

In our survey, we examine Jewish sources that relate to our topic. We shall mention the limitations imposed on acts that do harm to nature, one's neighbours, and society at large.

A number of the subjects we investigate are rooted in the laws governing relations among neighbours and the laws of torts. These laws are numerous and complex, and a comprehensive discussion of them all is far beyond the scope of the present survey. We shall, however, attempt to cover briefly a number of the guiding principles in these areas. And even if we do not find solutions for all the problems raised, we hope that we can at least refine the questions and pose challenges for further analysis of the issues.

Protecting Nature

1 Man and His Environment

I recall the early days, from 1905 onward, when it was granted me by the grace of the blessed Lord to go up to the holy land, and I came to Jaffa. There I first went to visit our great master R. Abraham Isaac Kook (of blessed memory), who received me with good cheer, as it was his hallowed custom to receive everyone. We chatted together on themes of Torah study. After the afternoon service, he went out, as was his custom, to stroll a bit in the fields and gather his thoughts; and I went along. On the way, I plucked some branch or flower. Our great master was taken aback; and then he told me gently, 'Believe me. In all my days I have taken care never to pluck a blade of grass or flower needlessly, when it had the ability to grow or blossom. You know the teaching of the Sages that there is not a single blade of grass below, here on earth, which does not have a heavenly force telling it Grow![10] Every sprout and leaf of grass says something, conveys some meaning. Every stone whispers some inner, hidden message in the silence. Every creation utters its song (in praise of the Creator).' Those words, spoken from a pure and holy heart, engraved themselves deeply on my heart. From that time on, I began to feel a strong sense of compassion for everything. (R. Aryeh Levine[11])

Rav Kook's attitude towards each individual plant and to the creation in general is based upon a comprehensive philosophical approach to man's relationship with nature. This position was well articulated by the noted mystic R Moshe Cordovero[12] in his work *Tomer Devorah*[13]:

One's mercy must extend to all the oppressed. One must not embarrass or destroy them, for the higher wisdom is spread over all that was created: inanimate, vegetable, animal, and human. For this reason were we warned against desecrating food stuVs... and in the same way, one must not desecrate anything, for all was created by His wisdom — nor should one uproot a plant, unless there is a need, or kill an animal unless there is a need.

2 *The Sabbatical Year*

The idea of conservation may be found in the biblical institution of the sabbatical year (*Lev.* 25:1–5):

And the Lord spoke unto Moses on Mount Sinai, saying: Speak unto the children of Israel, and say unto them: When you come into the land which I give you, then shall the land keep a sabbath unto the Lord. Six years shall you sow your field, and six years shall you prune you vineyard, and gather in the produce thereof. But in the seventh year shall be a sabbath of solemn rest for the land, a sabbath unto the Lord; you shall neither sow your field nor prune your vineyard. That which grows of itself of your harvest you shall not reap, and the grapes of your undressed vine you shall not gather; it shall be a year of solemn rest for the land.[14]

Maimonides[15], in his Guide for the Perplexed suggests a reason for the sabbatical year[16]:

With regard to all the commandments that we have enumerated in Laws concerning the Sabbatical year and the Jubilee, some of them are meant to lead to pity and help for all men – as the text has it: 'That the poor of the people may eat; and what they leave, the beasts of the field shall eat... ' (*Exod.* 23:11) –

and are meant to make the earth more fertile and stronger through letting it fallow.

In other words, one of the goals of ceasing all agricultural activity is to improve and strengthen the land.

Another reason for the sabbatical year which emphasises man's relationship with his environment is suggested by the author of Sefer haHinnukh in his explanation of the obligation to declare all produce ownerless (such that anyone may enter any field and take from its produce) during the sabbatical year[17]:

To the reasons for the Sabbatical Year, Rav Kook adds restoration of the proper balance among man, God, and nature. In the Sabbatical year, according to Rav Kook,

> … man returns to the freshness of his nature, to the point where there is no need to heal his illnesses, most of which result from destruction of the balance of life as it departs ever further from the purity of spiritual and material nature' (Introduction to Shabbat haAretz, pp. 8–9).

To establish in our hearts and make a strong impression on our thoughts that the world was created as a new entity out of nothing, 'that in six days God made the heaven and the earth' (*Exod.* 20:11);

> … and on the seventh day, when He created nothing, he decreed rest for Himself… And, therefore, the Holy One commanded [us] to declare all produce of the earth ownerless during this [sabbatical] year in addition to cessation of agricultural work, so that man will remember that the earth which yields its produce for him each year, does not do so on its own strength or of itself, but rather there is one who is Master over the land and its owners, and when He wishes, He commands that the produce be ownerless.

It is worth noting that the institution of the Sabbatical year is practiced into modern times within observant circles; the last Sabbatical observed was in 1993–94, (corresponding to the Hebrew calendar year 5754.)

3 *Altering Creation*

In addition to refraining from over-exploitation of the earth's resources, we must also be mindful of preserving the natural balance of creation. This is the approach taken by

R Avraham ibn Ezra[18] in his explanation of the biblical prohibition against mixing species. In *Leviticus* (19:19) we find:

> You shall keep my statutes. You shall not let your cattle gender with a diverse kind; you shall not sow your field with two kinds of seed; neither shall there come upon you a garment of two kinds of stuV mingled together.

One aspect of preventing changes in the creation finds expression in the effort to avoid causing the extinction of any animal. The presumption that everything that was created was created for some purpose denies us the possibility of eliminating from the world any species. So writes Nahmanides concerning the prohibition of mixing species[19]:

> The reason for the prohibition against mixing species is that God created all the species of the earth... and gave them the power to reproduce so that their species could exist forever, for as long as He wishes the world to exist, and He created for each one the capacity to reproduce its own species and not change it, forever... And this is the reason for sexual reproduction among animals, to maintain the species; so to among humans, it is for the purpose of being fruitful and multiplying[20].

See also TJ Kilayim 1:7 on *Lev.* 19:19: "You shall keep my laws' – the [natural] laws I have established in my world.' Cf. TB Kiddushin 39a; and Sanhedrin 60a. But *see Gen.* 1:26, '... and let them have dominion over the fish of the sea...'; and *Gen.* 1:28, and the comments of Nahmanides, ad loc., cited above, text to notes 3 and 5.

See also Sefer haHinnukh, commandment 244 (ed. Chavel, commandment 249), concerning the prohibition of breeding one species with another; and commandment 245 (ed. Chavel, commandment 250), concerning the prohibition of planting different species of seeds together.

4 *Wasteful Destruction*

a *The Prohibition of Wasteful Destruction*

An additional expression of man's obligation to preserve his natural environment may be found in the commandment against wasteful destruction, bal tash'hit. In general, the commandment prohibits the destruction of anything from which humans may benefit. It applies to the destruction of animals, plants, and even inanimate objects[21].

Instructive remarks are found in *Sefer haHinnukh's* discussion of the prohibition of cutting down fruit-bearing trees. The discussion opens with a discourse on the scope of the commandment[22]:

> We have been prevented from cutting down trees when we lay siege to a city in order to press and bring pain to the hearts of its residents, as is said, '... you shall not destroy the trees thereof... and you shall not cut them down' (*Deut.* 20:19). Included in this prohibition is destruction of every type, such as burning or tearing a garment, or breaking a vessel for no reason.

The author of Sefer haHinnukh then goes on to explain the reason for the prohibition:

> It is known that this commandment is meant to teach us to love the good and the useful and cling to them, and in this way goodness will cling to us, and we will avoid all that is bad and decadent. And this is the way of the pious: They love peace and rejoice in the good fortune of others, and bring everyone near to the Torah, and do not waste even a mustard seed, and they are pained by all destruction and waste that they see. And they save anything they can from destruction

with all their might. But the wicked are diVerent. They are the allies of those who destroy, they rejoice in destruction of the world and they destroy themselves: 'with the kind of measure a man measures, so shall he be measured ... (Mishnah Sot*ah* 1:7)'

The source of the prohibition of wasteful destruction is the biblical prohibition of cutting down fruit-bearing trees, which will be discussed below. The prohibition of wasteful destruction, however, is more comprehensive than the prohibition of destroying fruit-bearing trees, and it extends to anything that has use. In other words, the prohibition includes the destruction of man-made objects, and is not restricted to the preservation of nature.

b *Cutting Down Fruit-Bearing Trees*
In the book of *Deuteronomy* (20:19), among the laws concerning the waging of war, we find:

> When you shall besiege a city a long time, in making war against it to take it, you shall not destroy the trees thereof by wielding an axe against them; for you may eat of them, but you shall not cut them down; for is the tree of the field man, that it should be besieged by you?

The Bible thus warns that even in time of war, it is forbidden to destroy fruit-bearing trees.

The author[23] of *haKetav vehaKabbalah* explains the prohibition[24]:

> It is not proper to use some created thing for a purpose diametrically opposed to the purpose for which it was created, as has been stated[25] concerning *Exodus* 20:22: 'for if you lift up your sword to it, you have profaned it' – the altar was created to prolong the life of man, and iron was created to shorten the life of man; thus it is not fitting that something which shortens man's life be used upon that which lengthens it. So too a tree, which was created to make fruit to nourish men and animals, should have nothing done to it that destroys man.

c *For Man is a Tree of the Field*
The relationship of God, man, and nature is depicted in the biblical expression, 'For man is a tree of the field.'[26] Various interpretations have been given to this relationship: Even plants are subject to divine Providence; both man and the tree are God's creatures. Sifrei asserts[27], 'This shows that man's living comes from trees.'

The Sages also compared the death of the tree to the departure of man's soul from his body[28]:

> There are five sounds that go from one end of the world to the other, though they are inaudible. When people cut down the wood of a tree that yields fruit, its cry goes from one end of the world to the other, and the sound is inaudible... When the soul departs from the body, the cry goes forth from one end of the world to the other, and the sound is inaudible.[29]

On the basis of this passage, R Menahem Recanati[30] comments[31] that when man wreaks destruction in the material world, destruction is wreaked in the metaphysical world as well and that this is what was meant by 'For man is a tree of the field'.

Polluting the Environment

Smoking

Smoking constitutes a serious environmental pollutant and danger to health. Public awareness of this problem has led to legislation against smoking in public places[32].

Jewish legal authorities have considered whether it is prohibited to smoke in places where the smoke might bother others. One authority who absolutely prohibits smoking in public places is R Moshe Feinstein[33]. It is his opinion[34] that even if smoking were irritating only to those who are hypersensitive, it would nevertheless be prohibited to smoke in public places. Precedent for this holding is the talmudic case of R Yosef, who was hypersensitive[35] to noise. If it is possible to restrain particular actions on the basis of hypersensitivity, R Feinstein reasons, certainly it is possible to do so where there is pain or injury. Thus, where smoking is harmful to others, it is certainly prohibited[36].

Beauty

On seeing creatures that are beautiful or exceptionally well formed or goodly trees, one says, 'Blessed are You, O Lord our God, King of the universe who has such as these in His world.' If one goes out into the fields or gardens during the month of Nisan [i.e., the Spring] and sees the trees budding and the flowers in bloom, he says, Blessed are You, O Lord our God, King of the universe, who has made Your world lacking in nought and created therein beautiful creatures and goodly trees for the benefit of mankind.'[37]

Aesthetic beauty appears in Jewish sources not only as a value worthy of fostering in the life of the individual and the community, but also as the basis for a variety of legal obligations. The obligations derive from biblical regulations and from rabbinic legislation.

In the *Pentateuch* (Num. 35:2–5)[38], we find instructions regarding city planning, which required designation of open spaces free of all obstruction. Rashi describes the purpose of the open strip as being 'for the beautification of the city, that it have air'[39].

Later rabbinical legislation expanded the applicability of this rule to include cities other than those mentioned in the Bible[40].

Current Activities

The ideas of environmental protection and land conservation in the Jewish faith currently find application on a number of levels.

In Israel, the year 1994, was declared the 'Year of the Environment'. One of the many results of this declaration was that the environment was selected as the central theme of the Israeli educational system.

In honour of the Year of the Environment, the book *The Environment – Reflections and Perspectives in Jewish Sources*, was published. The book analyses the ideas of man's relation to the environment, as well as the vast legislative material in this area, from Scripture, the *Mishnah*, and *Talmud* (2nd–5th centuries) through the well known codifiers, such as Maimonides and the Shulhan Arukh, and the rich responsa literature. The booklet also traces how principles of environmental protection were given expression in ordinances passed in Jerusalem's new neighbourhoods constructed outside the city walls in the late nineteenth and early twentieth centuries.

Booklets on the Jewish sources concerning environmental protection were also prepared for use in the school system.

The Israeli legislature, the Knesset, enacted laws in such relevant areas as air and noise pollution, water pollution, recycling of waste, dangerous substances, protection of wildlife and vegetation, and establishment of nature preserves. It is the hope of the Jewish people that these activities further strengthen the awareness of environmental issues in Israel and throughout the world.

Summary

Man and Creation

The philosophical basis for man's relationship with his environment in general and the plant kingdom in particular was emphasised in early sources, in the *Midrash*, and in various philosophical works. The classic Jewish attitude to nature is a direct consequence of the belief that the entire universe is the work of the Creator. Love of God was taken in the broadest sense to include love of all His creations: the inanimate, plants, animals and man. Nature in all its beauty is understood as having been created for man, and it is, therefore, wrong for man to spoil it. Man's connection to nature can restore him to his original character, to a natural state of happiness and joy.

Balancing Interests

Protecting the environment involves protection of the natural balance, which includes, among other factors, the balance between man and the creation. But balance in this context does not mean equality. Balance may entail granting preference to man and his welfare, both physical and spiritual, and spiritual welfare may even take precedence over physical welfare. Conflicts of interest must be resolved by a careful weighing of values, a process that may sometimes result in absolute rejection of one value in favour of another. Nevertheless, in spite of man's preferred status, preservation of the environment need not necessarily be the value rejected. In some cases, it is man's interest that will be rejected in favour of the environment, particularly when the benefit to man is marginal, and damage to the environment is significant.

Man's Ownership is Not Absolute

Man's control over the world is restricted. 'For the earth is Mine' (*Lev.* 25:23) – only the Creator may be considered to enjoy absolute ownership of His creation. Man is commanded not to spoil the creation, but rather to improve and perfect it.

Man's rights in property are restricted. He may not use his possessions in ways likely to harm others. Principles were set forth for protecting the public domain, be it those areas 'owned' by the public or areas, such as the ozone layer that protects us from the harmful rays of the sun, which belong to no one but serve all.

Attitude toward Man

'Love thy neighbour as thyself' (*Lev.* 19:18), the basis for all Jewish ethics, is applied to protection of the environment in the obligation to exercise care not to harm others, and particularly in the obligation to avoid doing harm to the community. In proper relationships between man and his fellow man, and between man and his environment, the legal and ethical boundaries between 'mine' and 'not mine' become blurred.

Determining Legal Principles

In typical fashion, Jewish sources were not satisfied with merely emphasising 'environmental values', but also established concrete legal obligations. Jewish legal sources contain extensive discussion of the environmental issues that concern modern society, and point the way to protection against smoke, odours, pollution of air and water, and damage to the natural landscape.

Legal Perspectives

The basic principles of environmental protection, and the actions that flow from these principles, are based upon Scripture, and upon the reasons proposed for various commandments. The development of these principles continues in the post-biblical legal discourse of the *Mishnah, Talmud,* codes, and responsa.

In addition to various legal categories – such as torts – with implications for protection of the environment, both biblical law and subsequent legislation contain regulations aimed directly at environmental issues. Some of these restricted the rights of the individual vis-à-vis his environment, while others, on the contrary, extended his rights by permitting use of the public domain for personal needs. Special regulations were enacted for Jerusalem, owing to that city's unique status.

Extreme Forms of Nuisance

From the area of torts law, we learn of the serious view taken by the Sages toward damage to the environment.

Certain types of nuisance, such as smoke, foul odours, and noise, were classified as extreme, and those responsible for them were not permitted to claim 'unchallenged practice' in their defence. In such instances, the injured party's failure to protest does not establish the perpetrator's right to continue his offensive practice. Since the damage in these cases is to the injured party himself – not to his property – and causes him to suffer, the law presumes that he never waives his right to restrain the perpetrator. A similar principle operates for aesthetic values of the city, where residents do not have the power to waive enforcement of ordinances protecting aesthetic standards.

A person can be held responsible not only for direct damage to the environment. One who creates circumstances that lead to damage is also considered responsible. So, for instance, even if a person makes no noise himself, but rather creates a situation that causes noise to be produced, he can be restrained.

Even where compensation cannot be had, because the damage is indirect, the person who creates the circumstances that cause the damage can be compelled to desist.

Various activities and facilities must be located so as to prevent their doing damage to their surroundings. The distances specified in the *Mishnah* apply to conditions that pertained at the time of that work's compilation. As conditions change, however, distances must be adjusted accordingly.

Flexibility in Establishing Norms

Simple solutions do not exist for all problems. Just as in family law, where it is difficult to give precise definition to the types of behaviour that ought to result from the relationship of love and respect between man and wife, patterns of behaviour based upon love of nature and the creation cannot be readily translated into fixed, inflexible norms. Nevertheless, even where there is no set answer, the Sages developed criteria that can be applied to new and changing situations. Some questions will turn on the relative importance given to the welfare of the individual or the community on the one hand and environmental values on the other.

In mediating among competing values, the relative weight that should be assigned to the society's attitude to nature remains uncertain. It would seem important to ensure that there is not too great a gap between the attitude of the society and the obligations imposed by law, lest the demands be greater than the population can bear.

In our own time, the number of threats to the environment has increased greatly as a result of the growth of large urban centres and the development of industry. Smoke, industrial waste, untreated sewage, dumping sites in close proximity to residential areas, damage to the ozone layer, and various other ecological evils represent a real danger not only to the environment and the quality of life, but to life itself.

Today, the danger to the environment is many times greater than at any other time in history. Thus the increasing importance of the Jewish values and the approaches contained in Jewish legal sources. If the proper course is followed, man will not forfeit his opportunity to live a life of comfort in his environment, nor will the environment be uncomfortable with man.

Harmony In Four Parts
R. Avraham Yitzhak haKohen Kook

One man sings the song of his own soul, for it is there that his satisfaction is complete.
Another sings the song of his people, transcending the bounds of his own individual soul... cleaving with tender love to the Jewish people, singing her songs with her...
A third man's soul expands beyond the Jewish people to sing the song of man, his spirit embraces all humanity, majestic reflection of God...
And a fourth is transported still higher, uniting with the entire universe, with all creatures, and all worlds, with all of these does he sing... [41]

ENDNOTES

1. R. Avraham Yitzhak haKohen Kook (1865–1935) was the first chief rabbi of Palestine. Philosopher, scholar, legal authority, and mystic, he was one of the outstanding Jewish personalities of recent generations.

2. 'Hazon haTzimhonut vehaShalom, Afikim baNegev II,' in Lahai Ro'i, Yohanan Fried and Avraham Riger, eds., (Jerusalem, 1961), p. 207.

3. Berakhot 57b.

4. Mishnah Ketubot 13:10.

5. Ketubot 110b.

6. Rashi, ad loc., s.v. Yeshivat.

7. R. Yosi ben Hanina's opinion was codified as law: Maimonides, M.T., Ishut 13:17. *See also* Shul. Ar. Even haEzer 75:1.

8. Tosefta Baba Kama 2:10.

9. On the attitude to animals, *see* Nahum Rakover, Hagannat haHai (Tzed Hayyot), monograph no. 40 of Sidrat Mehkarim uSekirot baMishpat haIvri (Jerusalem, 1976).

10. *See* text to note 74 below.

11. R. Aryeh Levine was known as the 'prisoners' rabbi.' The passage appears in Simcha Raz, A Tzadik in Our Times, trans. Charles Wengrov (Jerusalem, 1976), pp. 108–109.

12. R. Moshe Cordovero (1522–1570) was the leading kabbalist of Safed in the period preceding R. Yitzhak Luria.

13. Tomer Devorah 3, ad fin.

14. *See also* Lev. 25:6–7; and Exod. 23:10–11.

15. Maimonides, R. Moshe ben Maimon (1135–1204), was born in Cordoba, Spain. He was the most distinguished Jewish authority of the Middle Ages.

16. Maimonides, The Guide of the Perplexed (trans. Shlomo Pines), III:39.

17. Sefer haHinnukh, commandment 84 (ed. Chavel, commandment 69). Cf. Sefer haHinnukh on the Jubilee Year, commandment 330 (ed. Chavel, commandment 326): 'God wished to teach His people that all belongs to Him, that ultimately all things are returned to the one to whom God wished to give them at the outset. For the world is His, as is written (Ex. 19:5), '... for all the earth is Mine."

18. R. Avraham ibn Ezra (ca. 1089–1164) was a biblical commentator, poet, philosopher, and physician. He lived in Spain.

19. Nahmanides, Lev. 19:19.

20. *See also* Nahmanides, Taryag Mitzvot haYotzim meAseret haDibrot, in Chaim Chavel, ed., Kitvei haRamban, vol. II, p. 544.

21. *See* Encyclopedia Talmudit, s.v. Bal tash'hit; Nahum Rakover, A Bibliography of Jewish Law – Otzar haMishpat, s.v. Bal tash'hit, vol. I, p. 285; vol. II, p. 278.

22. Sefer haHinnukh, commandment 529 (ed. Chavel, commandment 530).

23. R. Ya'akov Tzvi Mecklenberg (d. 1865), head of the rabbinic court of Koenigsberg.

24 haKetav vehaKabbalah, Deut. 20:19.

25 Mekhilta, Exod. 2:22; Rashi on the same verse.

26 Read as a statement rather than as a question.

27 Sifrei (ed. Finkelstein) 203.

28 Pirkei Rabbi Eliezer 34; *see also* commentary of R. David Luria, ad loc.

29 Just as there are sounds inaudible to human beings due to their high frequency, so the Sages know of additional sounds that humans are incapable of hearing.

30 R. Menahem Recanati was an early kabbalist active in Italy at the end of the thirteenth century and the beginning of the fourteenth century.

31 Commentary of Recanati, Shofetim. *See also* Yalkut meAm Lo'ez, Deut. 17.

32 In 1983, the Israeli Knesset enacted the Restriction of Smoking in Public Places Law, which was supplemented in 1994 by an executive order signed by the minister of health (Kovetz Takkanot, 21 July 1994, pp. 1197–98). The executive order confines smoking in the work place to specially designated areas where there are no non-smokers, where there is adequate ventilation, and smoking does not cause a nuisance to other parts of the work place.

33 R. Moshe Feinstein (1895–1986) was considered the spiritual leader of American Orthodoxy and American Jewry's leading authority on Jewish law in recent years.

34 *See* Resp. Iggerot Moshe, Hoshen Mishpat II:18.

35 *See* text to note 247 below.

36 *See* M. Halperin, 'haIshun – Sekirah Hilkhatit,' Asia, V (1986), 238–247; A. S. Avraham, Nishmat Avraham, Hoshen Mishpat 155:2; Dov Ettinger, Pe'er Tahat Efer – haIshun biYemei Hol uveYamim Tovim leOr haHalakhah (Jerusalem, 1989).

37 Maimonides, M.T., Berakhot 10:13.

38 *See also* Lev. 25:34.

39 Rashi, Sotah 27b, s.v. Migrash. Cf. Rashi's comments on Num. 35:2.

40 Maimonides, M.T., Shemitah veYovel 13:1–2, 4–5.

41 Orot haKodesh II, p. 444.

SIKHISM

after Sri Singh Sahib (Throne Of Timeless Being)

The whiteness of blossom,
And the witness of your presence
That is visible and invisible

Calling us to purify.

Bliss – to be in harmony with All Creation
In these seconds before you speak
Where something more than language, in the end,
Enters in:

Your two blue turbaned heads
Standing at the podium, side by side
– the Lamb with his friend the Lion,
Guarding and protecting the protected

As your fluent quiet speech unfolds:
And with all you say about how we see each other
What we leave to our children, and sacred temple land,
I see what you say as vibration

Where you come from the sky and the stars:

With the nightmare of the Punjab in front of you
Like the whole of the earth in miniature:
A dense black hole in a white canvas

Where you stand, like the White Rabbit Of God.*

* This is a personal image that denotes a total purity and vulnerability.
It is not a term of criticism.

Jay Ramsay

SIKHISM

Creating the world, God has made it a place to practise spirituality
(*Guru Granth Sahib*, p. 1035.)

THE SIKH scripture declares that the purpose of human beings is to achieve a blissful state and be in harmony with the earth and all creation. It seems, however, that humans have drifted away from that ideal. For the earth is today saturated with problems. It is agonising over the fate of its inhabitants and their future! It is in peril as never before. Its lakes and rivers are being choked killing its marine life. Its forests are being denuded. A smoky haze envelops the cities of the world. Human beings are exploiting human beings.

There is a sense of crisis in all parts of the world, in various countries and amongst various peoples. The demands of national economic growth and individual needs and desires are depleting the natural resources of the earth.

There is serious concern that the earth may no longer be a sustainable biosystem. The major crises facing the earth – the social justice crisis and the environmental crisis – together are heading the earth towards a disastrous situation. The social justice crisis is that of humanity's confrontation with itself and the environmental crisis is caused by humanity's confrontation with nature.

The social justice crisis is that poverty, hunger, disease, exploitation and injustice are widespread. There are economic wars over resources and markets. The rights of the poor and the marginal are violated. Women constituting half the world's population have their rights abused.

The environmental crisis caused by humanity's exploitation of nature is leading to the depletion of renewable resources, destruction of forests, over-use of land for agriculture and habitation. Today pollution is contaminating air, land and water. Smoke from industries, homes and vehicles is in the air. Industrial waste and consumer trash is affecting streams and rivers, ponds and lakes. Much of the waste is a product of modern technology; it is not bio-degradable, not re-usable and its long term consequences are unknown. The viability of many animal and plant species, and possibly that of the human species itself is at stake.

This crisis cries out for an immediate and urgent solution. The crisis requires a going back to the basic question of the purpose of human beings in this universe and an understanding of ourselves and God's creation.

We are called to the vision of Guru Nanak which is a World Society comprising God-conscious human beings who have realised God. To these spiritual beings the earth and the universe are sacred; all life is unity, and their mission is the spiritualisation of all.

Guru Nanak laid the foundation of Sikhism in the late fifteenth century. His writings, those of other human Gurus who succeeded him, and other spiritual leaders, are included in the scripture – *Guru Granth Sahib*. Guru Granth has been the Guru and Divine Master of the Sikhs since 1708, when Guru Gobind Singh declared that there would be no more human Gurus. Guru Nanak and his successors during their lifetime worked towards creating an ideal society that has as its basis spiritual awareness and ethical integrity. The name 'Sikh' means disciple or learner of the Truth.

Guru Nanak in his philosophy states that the reality that humans create around themselves is a reflection of their inner state. The current instability of the natural system of the earth – the external environment of human beings, is only a reflection of the instability and pain within humans. The increasing barrenness of the earth's terrain is a reflection of the emptiness within humans.

The solution to problems manifest in our world lies in prayer and accepting God's *hukam*. It is difficult to translate certain Sikh concepts accurately. *Hukam* is one such concept – it may be best described as a combination of God's will, order, or system. With an attitude of humility, and surrender to the Divine Spirit, conscientious human beings can seek to redress the current crises of the environment and of social justice. In the Sikh Way this is done through the guidance of the Guru, who is the Divine Master and messenger of God.

A Sikh theologian, Kapur Singh, explains that Sikhism has three postulates implicit in its teachings:

1 That there is no essential duality between spirit and matter.

2 That humans have the capacity to consciously participate in the process of spiritual progression.

3 The highest goal of spiritual progression is harmony with God, while remaining earth-conscious, so that the world itself may be transformed to a spiritual plane of existence.

Unity of Spirit and Matter and the Interconnectedness of all Creation
The Sikh view is that spirit and matter are not antagonistic. Guru Nanak declared that the spirit was the only reality and matter is only a form of spirit.

Spirit takes on many forms and names under various conditions.

> When I saw truly, I knew that all was primeval.
> Nanak, the subtle (spirit) and the gross (material) are, in fact, identical.
> (*Guru Granth Sahib*, p. 281)

That which is inside a person, the same is outside; nothing else exists;

> By divine prompting look upon all existence as one and undifferentiated;
> The same light penetrates all existence.
> (*Guru Granth Sahib*, p. 599)

The chasm between the material and the spiritual is in the minds of humans only. It is a limitation of the human condition that spirit and matter appear as duality, and their unity is not self-evident.

The material universe is God's creation. Its origin was in God and its end is in God; and it operates within God's *hukam*. Guru Nanak declares that God alone knows the reasons for and the moment of earth's creation. The origin of the universe is unknowable. The act of creation itself, the creation of the primeval atom, was instantaneous, caused by the Will of God.

Further descriptions of the universe and its creation in Sikh scripture are remarkably similar to recent scientific speculation about the universe and its origin. One of the basic hymns in the Sikh Scripture, which may be called the 'Hymn of the Genesis', describes the indeterminate void before the existence of this universe. (Appendix 1) Guru Nanak speaks of innumerable galaxies, of a limitless universe, the boundaries of which are beyond human ability to comprehend. God alone knows the extent of creation. (Appendix 3)

God created the universe and the world, for reasons best known to Him. And being the results of God's actions all parts of the universe are holy. God is an all-pervasive being manifest through various elements of creation. (Appendix 4)

Having created this universe and the world, God directs them. All actions take place within God's *hukam*. God alone knows how and why. God, however, not only directs this vast and massive theatre, but also watches over with care and kindness – the benign, supportive parent!

> Men, trees, pilgrimage places, banks of sacred streams, clouds, fields.
> Islands, spheres, universes, continents, solar systems.
> The sources of creation, egg-born, womb-born, earth-born,
> sweat-born, oceans, mountains and sentient beings.
> He, the Lord, knows their condition, O Nanak.
> Nanak, having created beings, the lord takes care of them all.
> The creator who created the world, He takes thought of it as well.
> (*Guru Granth Sahib*, p. 466)

The world, like all creation, is a manifestation of God. Every creature in this world, every plant, every form is a manifestation of the Creator. Each is part of God and God is within each element of creation. God is the cause of all and He is the primary connection between all existence.

> The Creator created himself...
> And created all creation in which he is manifest.
> You Yourself the bumble-bee, flower, fruit and the tree.
> You Yourself the water, desert, ocean and the pond.
> You Yourself are the big fish, tortoise and the Cause of causes.
> Your form can not be known.
> (*Guru Granth Sahib* p. 1016)

In the world God has created he has also provided each species and humans with means of support and nurturing.

In Sikh beliefs, a concern for the environment is part of an integrated approach to life and nature. As all creation has the same origin and end, humans must have consciousness of their place in creation and their relationship with the rest of creation. Humans should conduct themselves through life with love, compassion and justice. Becoming one and being in harmony with God implies that humans endeavour to live in harmony with all of God's creation.

The second postulate is that humans, practising a highly disciplined life, while remaining active in the world, are capable of further spiritual progression. It is important that Sikhs retain the primacy of spirit over matter, while it is desirable that they do not deny matter or material existence. It is not required that humans renounce the world. They must maintain their life in the world and uphold all responsibilities in the world. Humans should be renouncers of plenty and maintain a simple life. Further spiritual progress fundamentally starts with an individual conquering himself/herself with the guidance of the Guru. (Appendix 6) The emphasis is on mastery over the self and the discovery of the self; not mastery over nature, external forms and beings. Sikhism teaches against a life of conspicuous, wasteful consumption. The Guru recommends a judicious utilisation of material and cultural resources available to humans.

> Then why get attached to what you will leave behind.
> Having wealth, you indulge in pleasures bout,
> From that, tell me, who will bail you out?
> All your houses, horses, elephants and luxurious cars,
> They are just pomp and show, all totally false.
> (*Guru Granth Sahib*)

The Gurus taught humans to be aware of and respect the dignity in all life, whether human or not. Such a respect for life can only be fostered where one can first recognise the Divine spark within oneself, see it in others, cherish it, nurture and fulfil it.

> This little shrine of the human body!
> This great opportunity of life!
> The object is to meet the Beloved, thy Master!
> (*Guru Granth Sahib*)

Spiritual Discipline

Humans have the capability to further their spiritual progression through conscious choice and it is important to identify the method by which they might do so. The method suggested by Guru Nanak is one of spiritual discipline, meditation and prayer, and sharing. Sikhism emphasises mastering five negative forces: Lust, Anger, Worldly or Materialistic Attachment, Conceit and Greed. These together constitute what Sikhs term *Haumai* – 'I am-ness.' Mastering haumai is achieved by developing five positive forces: Compassion, Humility, Contemplation, Contentment and Service (seva) without expecting any material or spiritual reward. The guiding principles are Love and Forgiveness. Every decision in life has to be based on Rationality and a personal code of ethics. Guru Nanak's philosophy of values inspires the individual to transcend his/her existence through this spiritual discipline. Sikh religion preaches strong family involvement. A person pursuing this spiritual discipline must also work to create an atmosphere for other members of the family to progress spiritually.

The ideal Sikh – *someone who has an intense desire to do good*

The third postulate is that the true end of the human beings is in their emergence as God-conscious beings, who remain aware of the earth and operate in the mundane material world, with the object of transforming and spiritualising it into a higher plane of existence. In this spiritual state individuals are motivated by an intense desire to do good, transforming their surroundings.

Through a life based on the method prescribed by the Gurus humans may achieve a higher spiritual state. Such truly emancipated, valiant and enlightened spirits (*jivan-mukta, brahma-gyani*) become the true benefactors of humanity and the world around them. Such an individual would not exploit another human or sentient being, as each is a manifestation of the eternal and the supreme. In this God-conscious state they see God in all and everything.

> I perceive Thy form in all life and light;
> I perceive Thy power in all spheres and sight.
> (*Guru Granth*, p. 464)

Spiritualisation is a liberation from material compulsions and attractions. It means an awareness of the Cosmic Order and striving towards the execution of Divine Will. So, the spiritualised human is creative and constructive. Therefore a Sikh life is a life of harmony with other individuals with other beings and other forms. For an enlightened individual the world has only one purpose – to practise spirituality. That is the ultimate objective of all humans.

Such a person is involved in human problems and society and has to prove his or her effectiveness there. Such a person lives with a mission – and works for the emancipation of all. A true Sikh is for individual human rights, the environment, and justice for all.

The God-conscious person is animated with an intense desire to do good in this world.' (*Guru Granth Sahib*, p. 273)

Practising the Philosophy

Integrated Approach: Care of the Environment without Social Justice is not possible
Environmental concerns may be viewed as part of the broader issue of human development and social justice. Many environmental problems, particularly the exploitation of environmental resources in developing nations are due to the poverty of large parts of the population. Therefore an integrated approach is necessary.

Sikhism opposes the idea that the human race's struggle is against nature and its supremacy lies in the notion of 'harnessing' nature. The objective is harmony with the eternal – God – which implies a life of harmony with all existence. Striving for a life of harmony, therefore, also implies a life of supporting individual rights, environmentalism, – a life that works against injustice towards anybody and anything.

The tenth Guru founded the Order of the Khalsa in 1699, who practise the spiritual discipline of Sikhism, and are committed to ensure the preservation and prevalence of a World Society. Over the last three centuries the members of the Khalsa order have stood up for the rights of the oppressed and the disenfranchised even at the cost of their own lives. The Khalsa vision of the World Society is:

> Henceforth such is the Will of God:
> No man shall coerce another;
> No person shall exploit another.
> Each individual, has the inalienable birth-right
> to seek and pursue happiness and self-fulfilment.
> Love and persuasion is the only law of social coherence.
> (*Guru Granth Sahib*, p. 74)

The Khalsa have opposed any force that has threatened the freedom and dignity of human beings. In the eighteenth century it was the oppressive rulers of northern India, and invaders from Afghanistan; in the nineteenth and twentieth centuries they have struggled against the oppression of European colonists and Indian governments. For the Khalsa justice requires the participation and inclusion of all in obtaining and enjoying the fruits of God's creation. Justice achieved through co-operative effort is desirable. The ideal for the Khalsa is to strive for justice for all, not merely for themselves.

The Institution of Sangat, Pangat and Langar
The Sikh Gurus, through their lives provided role models for the Sikhs. They all actively worked to stress the equality of all humans and challenged the rigid

social stratification of the caste system in India. The very existence of the Sikh religion is based on challenging

1 inequality in society, and
2 the exploitation of the poor and the marginal by the religious and political establishment.

Sikh Gurus provided many examples of standing by their principles and confronting exploitation and oppression. They stood by the 'low' and the 'poor', for, as Guru Nanak said:

> There are the lowest men among the low-castes.
> Nanak, I shall go with them. What have I got to do with the great?
> God's eye of mercy falls on those who take care of the lowly.
> (*Guru Granth Sahib*, p. 15)

Sikh Gurus challenged the status quo and came into conflict with the entrenched elite – political, social, religious and economic. The Gurus were most sympathetic to the down-trodden of society, the untouchables and those of lower caste. They vehemently opposed the division of society on the basis of caste, which had been and is still significantly present. They identified themselves with the poor in full measure and were critical of those responsible for their misery. In the course of their travels they preferred to live in the homes of those who made an honest living to the homes of the rich who thrived on exploitation.

Two Sikh Gurus were martyred by the regimes of their period for challenging the contemporary authorities. One, Guru Tegh Bahadur was martyred when he stood up for the religious freedom of the Hindu inhabitants of Kashmir who were being forced to accept Islam by the rulers.

Sikh Gurus also moulded traditional lifestyles to exemplify a more equitable society. They created many institutions that form the basis of Sikh society and are based on the equality of all. The Sikh Gurus invited people of all castes and creed to meditate together. That would be called *Sangat*. Either before or after the meditation, people were asked to sit and eat together irrespective of their social background to create a sense of equality. That process would be called *Pangat*. Sikh Gurus started a tradition of free distribution of food to the rich or poor through the Sikh meeting areas. That would be called *Langar*. These three ideas were in contrast to the Indian society which had separate temples or water wells for social outcasts. These changes by the Sikh Gurus created a lot of opposition from the religious establishment. These changes are still much alive in Sikh practices today. Through the creation of the Khalsa, the Gurus established a system which would protect and maintain a free and just order.

Equality of women

Women and their rights have been ignored for too long. Any approach to solve problems of social justice and the environment must be sensitive to women's concerns, and must include women as equals.

Often piece-meal solutions to environmental problems focus on limiting population growth and family planning programmes. Most family planning measures end up abusing women's rights and should be rejected on those grounds alone. Meanwhile they spread mistrust of family planning among women.

Guru Nanak and other Sikh Gurus in their life advocated equality and dignity to women and took steps to implement these principles. Guru Nanak denounced the idea that spirituality was only for men, and not for women. The first Sikh Guru in his preaching and writings made direct statements emphasising that women were no less than men:

> After the death of one's wife, one seeks another,
> and through her social bonds are cemented.
> Why should we condemn women who give birth to leaders and rulers?
> Everyone is born of a woman and a woman alone.
> Nobody is born otherwise.
> God alone is an exception to this rule.
> (*Guru Granth Sahib*, p. 473)

Guru Amardas strongly opposed the custom of *Sati* in the sixteenth century and also advocated widow marriages. *Sati* was the Indian practice whereby widows burned themselves with their husband's corpse at cremation. Guru Amar Das appointed and ordained a large number of women preachers, and at least one bishop – Mathura Devi, four hundred years ago. The Sikh Gurus also raised their voice against the Purdah or veil. Guru Amardas did not even allow the Queen of Haripur to come into the religious assembly wearing a veil.

The immediate effect of these reforms was that women gained an equal status with men. Those who lived as grovelling slaves of society became fired with a new hope and courage to lift themselves to be equals of the best in humanity. The spirit of the Sikh woman was raised with the belief that she was not a helpless creature but was a responsible being endowed with a will of her own with which she could do much to mould the destiny of society.

Women came forward as the defenders of their honour and dignity. They also became the rocks that stood against tyrants. Without the burden of unnecessary and unreasonable customs, Sikh women became the temporal and spiritual supporters of men, often acting as the 'conscience of men'. Sikh women proved themselves as the equals of men in service, devotion, sacrifice and bravery.

Since the late nineteenth century, Sikh community organisations have made efforts at expanding educational opportunities for all. Individual Sikhs, men and women, in various cities and towns, took the initiative to start and operate women's colleges and schools. Women's education was part of the drive to improve education among the Sikhs, initiated by Sikh organisations in the 1920s.

In towns and villages in the Punjab, and in cities with significant Sikh populations, there exist schools and colleges operated by Sikh organisations.

Community-based Sharing of Resources

Traditional modes of farming, and traditional modes of life in Northern India have been dependent upon limited resources. As there exist circumstances where there are large numbers of people dependent upon relatively limited resources, the traditional lifestyle ensures use of the least resources, considerable re-use, and recycling of resources. In a culture based on organic resources and materials, recycling is an intrinsic and natural part of the resource cycle. There are strong traditions of sharing resources.

There have been traditional practices that maintained lands and forests as community property within proximity of human habitation. For instance in traditional rural India and Punjab, two of the most important centres of human activity have been the Sikh *gurudwara*, and a source of water – pond, tank, pool or running water. Both of these sites were surrounded by community land, not owned by anyone and not used for agriculture. This was where there were trees and plants – groves or small forests. They provided shade and shelter, and were a source of firewood within easy reach of habitation.

The Gurus established towns and cities, each created around a religious centre. The focus was on a lifestyle based on sharing. A life style that promoted equity among people, and optimum utilisation of resources. Even today, even rural Punjab families share resources with their neighbours. This is particularly evident on large family occasions such as weddings, when the entire village may play host to guests and share living space, beds, etc.

Most *gurudwaras* in India were specifically designed to have a water tank, or were near running water (rivers or pools) – which were always considered a community resource. For instance, Amritsar grew up around the *Harimandir* (ordinarily referred to as the Golden Temple) and the *Amrit Sarovar* (the pool of nectar – the water). The cities and towns that grew around *gurudwaras* were ideally centred on a spiritual lifestyle based on sharing.

Since the time of the Gurus, Sikh *gurudwaras*, have included institutionalised practices that emphasise sharing of resources. *Gurudwaras*, in addition to being places for congregation for prayer and meditation, are (1) a place to stay for travellers and others; (2) a community kitchen – *langar*; (3) a place for dispensing medication and medical care; (4) a place to impart education to the young. *Gurudwaras* have always been places of shelter for travellers and visitors. Most major *gurudwaras* have rooms where visitors may stay. In addition Sikh *gurudwaras* stock extra beds, pots and pans, etc. At weddings and other family events, the *gurudwaras* are a source for borrowing sheets, beds, pots and pans.

There has always been great emphasis on avoiding waste. Traditionally the community kitchen served food on plates made from leaves and cups made from clay. Today they tend to use steel plates and utensils that are re-used. The kitchens have always been stocked by ordinary people – farmers, traders, others in the community – on a voluntary basis.

Sikhism against Smoking

It is now a known fact that smoking is both a primary and secondary health hazard. In addition to the environment, it has seriously deleterious effects on the person who smokes, to the bystander who breathes the secondhand smoke, and to the unborn fetus of the female smoker. Though this only been scientifically verified in the last half-century, Guru Gobind Singh, the last living Guru of the Sikhs listed the use of tobacco as one of the four major acts forbidden to initiated adherents of the Sikh region. Though tobacco was introduced into India only in the mid-1600s, he had the wisdom to specifically interdict it in 1699. From its very beginning, Sikhism had forbidden the use of any intoxicants or mind-altering substances for any purpose, except medicinal.

Conclusion

The ideal for Sikhism is a society based upon mutual respect and co-operation and providing an optimal atmosphere for individuals to grow spiritually. Sikhism regards a co-operative society as the only truly religious society, as the Sikh view of life and society is grounded in the worth of every individual as a microcosm of God. Therefore, an individual must never be imposed upon, coerced, manipulated or engineered:

> If thou wouldst seek God, demolish and distort not the heart of any individual (*Guru Granth Sahib*, p. 1384)

All life is interconnected. A human body consists of many parts, every one of them has a distinct name, location and function and all of them are dependent upon each other. In the same way, all the constituents of this universe and this earth are dependent upon each other. Decisions in one country or continent cannot be ignored by others. Choices in one place have measurable consequences for the rest of the world. It is part of the same system.

Life, for its very existence and nurturing, depends upon a bounteous nature. A human being needs to derive sustenance from the earth; not to deplete, exhaust, pollute, burn or destroy it. Sikhs believe that an awareness of that sacred relationship between humans and the environment is necessary for the health of our planet, and for our survival. A new 'environmental ethic' dedicated to conservation and wise use of the resources provided by a bountiful nature can only arise from an honest understanding and dedicated application of our old, tried and true spiritual heritage.

APPENDICES

1 'Through countless ages
Complete darkness prevailed;
In a complete void
There was no world, no firmament.
The Will of the Lord alone existed
Neither night nor day, neither sun nor moon;
Only God in an endless trance.
Neither creation, nor destruction, neither coming nor going;
There were no continents, no underworlds;
No seven oceans, no rivers, no flowing waters;
There were no higher, middle or lower planes;
Neither was there heaven, nor hell;
Neither death nor time;
There was no world of tortures, nor region of bliss;
Neither birth nor death;
When He so willed, Then He created the world,
and without any support sustained the firmament.
He founded the continents, solar systems, underworld,
and from the Absolute Self, he became manifest.
None knows his limit, It is through the True Teacher (Guru)
the secret is revealed.'
(*Guru Granth Sahib*, p. 1035)

2 'The forms become in according to Divine Will.
Human comprehension fails at this stage to understand the Divine Will.'
(*Guru Granth Sahib*, p. 1)

3 Guru Nanak describes:
'Hundreds of thousands of worlds beneath and over ours'
(*Guru Granth Sahib*, p. 3)

4 'True are Your Universes, and true are your solar systems,
True are Your Worlds and true Your Creation,
True are Your doings and all deliberations,
True is Your order and true Your courts.'
(*Guru Granth Sahib*, p. 438)

5 'Let truth be the strict norm of all you think and do, so that your pain and anxiety
may go and all-felicity come to you,
Always cognise the near presence of God, through the practice of the Name,
Avoid hurt or injury to any sentient being so that peace may come to your mind,
Be humble by helping and serving those afflicted with misery and want so as to
achieve God-consciousness
Nanak testifies that God is the exalter of the fallen and lowly.'
(*Guru Granth Sahib*, p. 322)

6 'Hail the Guru, for he teaches the ascent of man over himself'
(*Guru Granth Sahib*, p. 462)

7 'All nights all days all dates all occasions
All seasons, months, the entire Earth and all its load.
All Waters all winds, all the fires and underworlds.
All spheres, all divisions of Earth, and all worlds, men and forms.
How great is the Lord's command over them all cannot be known
Nor can the Lord's deeds be described.'
(*Guru Granth Sahib*)

8 'The air is deemed to be Guru, Water the father and the Earth our mother,
Whose belly gives us all the things.
Night and day are the two female and male nurses.
Made to play thus, the world plays in their lap.
You Yourself are the fish and yourself the net.
You Yourself are the cow and the grazer
Your light pervades in all the beings of the world just as lord has willed.'
(*Guru Granth*, p. 1021)

9 'One who realises the visible as merged in the formless.
And finds poise in the truth of God's invisible power–
Such a one shall not be subject to the cycle of births.'
(*Guru Granth Sahib*, p. 414)

10 'A godly person covets not any women except his legal wife.
His relations with other women are governed by profound respect.'
(*Guru Granth Sahib*)

This statement compiled under the guidance of:
Sri Singh Sahib Manjit Singh
Jathedar
Sri Akhal Takhat Sahib

TAOISM
for Grand Master Xie Zongxing

Chapter 32 of the *Tao Te Ching*

The Tao has no name
              it is a cloud that has no shape.
If a ruler
follows it faithfully,
then every living thing under heaven will say yes to him.

Heaven and earth make love,
And a sweet dew-rain falls.
The people do not know why,
But they are gathered together like music.

Things have been given names from the beginning.
We need to know when we have enough names: this is wisdom.

At the beginning of time
The sage gives names to everything – seen, and unseen.

A ruler who walks the Way
Is like a river reaching the sea
Gathering the waters of the streams
                          into himself,
        as he goes.

                              Translated by:
                              Man-Ho Kwok
                              Martin Palmer
                              Jay Ramsay

The chapter from the *Tao Te Ching* is taken from the Element Books
edition (1993).

诗色长于洒沙堡

TAOISM

*T*AOISM EMERGED on the basis of what are known as the One Hundred Schools of Thought during the period 770–221 BC. Starting with the formal setting up of Taoist organisations in the East Han period (25–220 AD), it has a history of nearly 2,000 years. Taoism has been one of the main components of Chinese traditional culture, and it has exerted great influence on the Chinese people's way of thinking, working and acting. It is no exaggeration to say that in every Chinese person's consciousness and subconsciousness, the factors of Taoism exist to a greater or lesser degree.

Because of its deep cultural roots and its great social impact, Taoism is now one of the five recognised religions in China; namely Buddhism, Christianity, Catholicism, Islam, and Taoism. Even more, the influence of Taoism has already transcended the Chinese-speaking world, and has attracted international attention.

According to our statistics, more than 1,000 Taoist temples have now opened to the public (this number does not include those in Taiwan, Hong Kong and Macao) and about 10,000 Taoists live in such communities. There are about 100 Taoist associations all over China, affiliated to the China Taoist Association. Several colleges have also been established to train Taoists, and many books and periodicals on the study and teaching of Taoism have been published. All Taoists work hard in order that Taoism should develop and flourish. They take an active part in mobilising the masses, carrying forward the best in Taoist tradition and working for the benefit of human society.

Like every major world religion, Taoism has its own outlook on the universe, human life, ideals of virtue and ultimate purpose. Due to its distinctive cultural and historical background, it has its own striking characteristics. It can be briefly summarised in the following two precepts:

1. *Give respect to the Tao above everything else*
Tao simply means 'the way'. Taoism considers that Tao is the origin of every-

thing, and Tao is the ultimate aim of all Taoists. This is the most fundamental tenet of Taoism. Tao is the way of Heaven, Earth and Humanity. The Tao took form in the being of the Grandmother Goddess. She came to Earth to enlighten humanity. She taught the people to let everything grow according to its own course without any interference. This is called the way of no-action, no-selfishness (*wu-wei*), and this principle is an important rule for Taoists. It teaches them to be very plain and modest, and not to struggle with others for personal gain in their material life. This kind of virtue is the ideal spiritual kingdom for which the followers of Taoism long.

2 *Give great value to life*

Taoism pursues immortality. It regards life as the most valuable thing. Master Chang Daoling (*c.* 2nd century AD) said that life is another expression of Tao, and the study of Tao includes the study of how to extend one's life. With this principle in mind, many Taoists have undertaken considerable exploration in this regard. They believe that life is not controlled by Heaven, but by human beings themselves. People can prolong life through meditation and exercise. The exercises include both the moral and the physical sides. People should train their will, discard selfishness and the pursuit of fame, do good deeds, and seek to become a model of virtue (*te*).

Taoism considers that the enhancement of virtue is the precondition and the first aim of practising the Tao. The achievement of immortality is a reward from the gods for practising worthy acts. With a high moral sense and with systematic exercise in accordance with the Taoist method and philosophy of life, people can keep sufficient life essence and energy in their bodies all their lives. The Taoist exercise of achieving immortality has proved very effective in practice. It can keep people younger and in good health. But there is one point which cannot be neglected: a peaceful and harmonious natural environment is a very important external condition.

Taoist Ideas about Nature

With the deepening world environmental crisis, more and more people have come to realise that the problem of the environment is not only brought about by modern industry and technology, but it also has a deep connection with people's world outlook, with their sense of value and with the way they structure knowledge. Some people's ways of thinking has, in certain ways, unbalanced the harmonious relationship between human beings and nature, and overstressed the power and influence of the human will. People think that nature can be rapaciously exploited.

This philosophy is the ideological root of the current serious environmental and ecological crisis. On the one hand, it brings about high productivity; on the other hand, it brings about an exaggerated sense of one's own importance. Confronted with the destruction of the Earth, we have to conduct a thorough self-examination on this way of thinking.

We believe that Taoism has teachings which can be used to counteract the shortcomings of currently prevailing values. Taoism looks upon humanity as the most intelligent and creative entity in the universe (which is seen as encompassing humanity, Heaven, Earth within the Tao).

There are four main principles which should guide the relationship between humanity and nature:

1   In the *Tao te Ching*, the basic classic of Taoism, there is this verse: 'Humanity follows the Earth, the Earth follows Heaven, Heaven follows the Tao, and the Tao follows what is natural.' This means that the whole of humanity should attach great importance to the Earth and should obey its rule of movement. The Earth has to respect the changes of Heaven, and Heaven must abide by the Tao. And the Tao follows the natural course of development of everything. So we can see that what human beings can do with nature is to help everything grow according to its own way. We should cultivate in people's minds the way of no-action in relation to nature, and let nature be itself.

2   In Taoism, everything is composed of two opposite forces known as Yin and Yang. Yin represents the female, the cold, the soft and so forth: Yang represents the male, the hot, the hard and so on. The two forces are in constant struggle within everything. When they reach harmony, the energy of life is created. From this we can see how important harmony is to nature. Someone who understands this point will see and act intelligently. Otherwise, people will probably violate the law of nature and destroy the harmony of nature.

There are generally two kinds of attitude towards the treatment of nature, as is said in another classic of Taoism, *Bao Pu Zi* (written in the 4th century AD). One attitude is to make full use of nature, the other is to observe and follow nature's way. Those who have only a superficial understanding of the relationship between humanity and nature will recklessly exploit nature. Those who have a deep understanding of the relationship will treat nature well and learn from it. For example, some Taoists have studied the way of the crane and the turtle, and have imitated their methods of exercise to build up their own constitutions. It is obvious that in the long run, the excessive use of nature will bring about disaster, even the extinction of humanity.

3   People should take into full consideration the limits of nature's sustaining power, so that when they pursue their own development, they have a correct

standard of success. If anything runs counter to the harmony and balance of nature, even if it is of great immediate interest and profit, people should restrain themselves from doing it, so as to prevent nature's punishment. Furthermore, insatiable human desire will lead to the over-exploitation of natural resources. So people should remember that to be too successful is to be on the path to defeat.

4   Taoism has a unique sense of value in that it judges affluence by the number of different species. If all things in the universe grow well, then a society is a community of affluence. If not, this kingdom is on the decline. This view encourages both government and people to take good care of nature. This thought is a very special contribution by Taoism to the conservation of nature.

To sum up, many Taoist ideas still have positive significance for the present world. We sincerely hope that the thoughts of all religions which are conducive to the human being will be promoted, and will be used to help humanity build harmonious relationships between people and nature. In this way eternal peace and development can be maintained in the world.

China Taoist Association,
White Cloud Temple,
Beijing, 1995

ONENESS
in the Holy Spirit of Love

Start at the end: spirit and matter are the same
And all faiths point to the same blindness

What is that blindness? Light
And our incomprehension of beauty

It swings us off our feet
To take one drop of it into the heart

Its other name is Love, what we fall in
Through all the walls, into ourselves as we are.

Love is the only answer – love for real
Breaking in between all of us...

And there is a dancer who will lead us there:
His name is Resurrection –

                              Hers is Joy

And theirs is ours, as mine is yours.

Jay Ramsay

PART THREE

CARING FOR HOLY GROUND

Examples of Practice from Around the World

OVERHEARD ON THE TRAIN
Waterloo to Windsor, BR

'I can't be bothered to recycle', she said
With her black perm and Mrs. Mouse voice –
'Because every time I go it's all over the floor'

And I want to say 'Yes, madam, that's the mess we're in
And are you going to help us pick up the pieces?'

★

Leaving London: the grey giving way to the green,
The blossoming sidings and the astro-grafitti

Two realities: one dreaming, one growingly real
One all over the Internet of the Intercity night
The other taking the time of day

The time we save that we are saved in
That finally opens in the Rose...

★

(We draw up right by a recycling ad.
　　　　　　She doesn't seem to notice it.)

★

'We have a lilac tree lying down in our garden'
Says white perm –
'It's been there ever since we have – since '87'
Ah yes, the hurricane, the levelling
– as they all fall silent momentarily –

Outside, the pylons and the ploughed-up fields
And the whole land straining to break free and *be*.

Jay Ramsay

INTRODUCTION

*A*LL THE fine statements in the world add up to nothing if they do not materialise into action. From
the days of Assisi onwards, religions and conservation
groups have been working together to make the teachings realities. Hundreds of thousands of religious projects
on the environment now exist and they are growing daily.
In 1986, it was hard to find any religious leader who felt
that the environment was of central significance to their
faith. Today it is commonplace that this is so. This is in
some degree a sign of the success of this programme of
work by WWF.

In the final section of this book we look at practical
projects and at models being developed such as the Ohito
Declaration. Models which encourage others to take action.

In the end, this is what matters. What you do is shaped
by what you believe. In the collaboration of religions
with conservation groups, this is taking place every day,
world wide.

PROJECTS

*E*ACH OF the religions has sought to give practical expression to their beliefs about nature through a range of conservation and environmental education projects. While all religions have developed projects, some have been more committed to such work than others. This section contains a sample of the many initiatives that are now operating throughout the world.

Bahá'í

International Tree Planting Campaigns
Short and long-term tree-planting campaigns have been initiated by Bahá'í communities in many places across the planet: these include the Breath of Life tree-planting project of the Bahá'í community of Hawaii which planted indigenous trees on all the Hawaiian Islands; the reforestation efforts of the students of the Rabbani Bahá'í High School in Madhya Pradesh, India, where tens of thousands of trees have been planted around the campus and in neighbouring villages; the efforts of Bahá'ís in Washington, United States, to replant denuded stream banks; the villages reforestation project of the Anís Zunúzí Bahá'í School in Port au Prince, Haiti; and the campaign of the Bahá'ís of Iceland to plant thousands of trees on Skógar, the ancestral property of the famous Icelandic poet, Mr Jochum M Eggertsson.

Buddhism

Cambodia: Shante Sena Forestry Association
Over the past 20 years the amount of forest cover in Cambodia has fallen from 73 per cent to less than 40 per cent. To search for solutions to this grave problem, the Shante Sena Forestry Association, led by the Venerable Nhem Kin Teng, has begun a community-based forestry project which integrates Buddhist and traditional beliefs.

The Shante Sena (Peace Army) educates local villagers and Buddhist monks and nuns to join tree-planting conservation programmes. In 1994, thirty volunteers were educated and trained at workshops in community forestry, Buddhism and non-violence.

Since the Shante Sena was formed, 150,000 trees have been planted in the Chantrea district of Svay Rieng, where forests had been destroyed. It has educated villagers in temples, schools and households about the importance of protecting their natural resources and the links between environmental destruction and the irregular rains. Because of Shante Sena's concern for environmental conservation, they were recently able to register as an NGO (Non-Governmental Organisation) with the Cambodian government.

UK: Holy Island Project

Holy Island is situated in the firth of Clyde, just east of the Isle of Arran. It has always been a place of great religious significance and contains a number of sacred sites, including the cave of St Molaise, a 6th century hermit, and the ruins of a 13th century monastery.

In 1992, the island was bought by the Samye Ling Tibetan Centre, who aim to build on this sacred heritage by establishing a Buddhist retreat centre in a self-sustaining environment. A number of conservation projects have now been set up on the island and over 27,000 trees have been planted.

The retreat centre itself is being built to blend in with the surounding environment. It will be partly dug into a hillside and its roof will be covered with earth. It is also designed to be self-sufficient in both heat and water.

The project has been underatken in collaboration with the Alliance of Religions and Conservation and is a forerunner to the Sacred Land Project, to be launched in 1997 (see p. 137).

Christianity

Greece: Mount Athos Environmental Programme

Mount Athos is situated on a Greek peninsula 60 km in length and covers an area of approximately 360 square kilometres. At the tip of the peninsula is Mount Athos itself, whose summit rises sheer from the sea to 2,000 metres. For many centuries this has been a centre of monastic life for the Orthodox Church and on Athos today there are twenty monasteries, twelve dependencies and several hermitages. Because of centuries of relative isolation, Mount Athos has a unique cultural and natural landscape.

Recently, however, concern has been expressed about the deterioration of its natural environment due to the escalating number of visitors to the peninsula, and the changing pattern of land management resulting in increased road building.

Under a joint project sponsored and supported by WWF International and the Ecumenical Patriarchate of Constantinople, a survey of the monasteries on Mount Athos was conducted, with regard to their landholdings, environmental management and conservation issues.

Following the survey major environmental projects have begun on the lands of the Holy Mountain, supported by WWF Greece. These projects include:

The preservation of 250 hectares at the monastery of Pantokrator – part of the largest remaining undisturbed Mediterranean forest in the whole of the eastern Mediterranean.

The declaration of the whole end of the Athonite Peninsula as a nature reserve.

The monastery of the Grand Lavra to use Piperi and Skantzoura, its islands in the Aegean, as a sanctuary for monk seals.

The introduction of the principles of organic farming to the management of the extensive agricultural properties around the the Convent of Ormlylia near Thessaloniki in northern Greece.

(The convent is not on Mount Athos but is a dependent of the monastery of Simonopetra on Mount Athos.)

UK: The Sacred Land Project

In the various forms of Chrisianity that have emerged in Britain, there is a long tradition of valuing the natural world as an expression of God's love. Prior to this, the older religious traditions saw themselves as being part of nature.

The importance of valuing the land from a religious perspective seems, however, to have been ignored or lost by many. There is a widespread and growing sense that there needs to be a rediscovery, a change in our modern underlying attitude towards the land in order to prevent and redress environmental damage and neglect.

Throughout Britain there are thousands of shrines, wells, pilgrimage routes and other features of the landscape which have for centuries been regarded as special or sacred. Some of these are still a focus of pilgrimage or festival and attract many visitors, but the history and significance of many has been lost or forgotten.

The Sacred Land project is a five year scheme (April 1997–March 2002) run by WWF-UK in partnership with ICOREC, which aims to re-establish the spiritual and environmental significance of these sites and to keep alive the tradition of sacred space in today's society in both rural and urban settings.

The project will seek to revive and celebrate the sacred meaning and significance of sites by:

Rediscovering and reopening old pilgrimage routes and finding environmentally sensitive ways of managing those routes as well as creating new routes, e.g. a multi-faith pilgrimage across Britain.

Rediscovering the sacred designs of many medieval cities and towns, such as Bristol, and working from those to revive the beauty of the built landscape.

Reopening, restoring, and creating urban and rural sacred spaces and managing them as places of natural beauty, peace and healing, such as the 8th century shrine of St. Melangell in North Wales or a Path of Life sacred garden on a housing estate in Manchester.

Managing, and where necessary, replanting wooded areas which belong to historical monuments, abbeys, and churches.

Re-establishing and creating herbal gardens in cathedrals and churchyards.

A number of books are being published in conjunction with the project, including *A Guide to Sacred Britain* (Piatkus, 1997) and *Sacred Journeys* (Gaia Books, 1997).

Hinduism

India: The Vrindavan Conservation Project

Vrindavan, the pastoral playground of Krishna, has been one of the most important pilgrimage centres of India from the 15th century to the present day. Every devout follower of Krishna wishes to visit or settle down in Krishna's land, with the result that today the beautiful groves and gardens have been sacrificed for temples housing Krishna and homes for his devotees. This pressure on the environment was not compensated for, and the essential needs of water, sanitation, traffic control, and maintaining the green surroundings have taken a terrible beating.

At the request of some of the Vrindavan community, WWF India began working with Vrindavan's people in 1991, focusing on greening the 11 km sacred pilgrimage route (*parikrama*) around the town. Over 2,000 traditional trees and flowering bushes have been planted, and dedicated efforts have been made to overcome the initial indifference of the community and civic authorities. Two plant nurseries have been established, and over 10,000 saplings of religious fruit and flowering trees, sacred creepers, and bushes have been distributed to residents and *ashrams*. Two small parks have been created; WWF helped obtain the water connection from the administration, and members of the community – including and especially children – dug the water tank and provided fencing for the trees.

Friends of Vrindavan

Friends of Vrindavan (FoV) is a North/South partnership which believes that conservation has to take place equally on both sides of the North/South divide. In 1992 the community in Leicester, UK, established Friends of Vrindavan to support the conservation work in Vrindavan and to create interest in the natural ecology of Vrindavan within Leicester. This has led to practical environmental projects such as the creation of a 'Vrindavan Gardens' in Central Leicester, currently being undertaken by the Leicester Hindu community, with help from the City Council.

Islam

Jordan: Al al-Bayt University Projects

Al al-Bayt University is an International Islamic University which has been established by the order of His Majesty King Hussein of Jordan and chaired by HRH Crown Prince Hussan, brother of the King. The University focuses on the international dimension of Islam and other religions and functions as a cross-cultural meeting place at which people (staff and students) of different origins and religions can be brought together to extend and enhance their understanding of each others' cultural background on the basis of global vision and spiritual values. The environment and conservation are also major concerns of the university, particularly as the university is built in an area which was exposed to deforestation during the First World War and which is now classified as a semi-arid zone.

The University is conducting projects in the areas of reforestation, conservation and bio-diversity, water management, waste water treatment. It also runs a prorgamme of Environmental Education and is researching and producing a publication which compares modern sciences' understanding of 'the environment' with the teachings to be found in the Holy Qur'an.

Jainism

India: Veersevadal (VSD) Community Youth Project

VSD started as a non-political organisation of young people primarily to develop discipline, self-respect and awareness of social and ecological responsibilities. The word *veer* comes from the teaching of Mahavira (*c.*500 BCE) and means 'live and let live', while *seva* means 'the donation of time and services without the expectation of any personal rewards'.

VSD promotes vegetarianism, anti-drug movements and afforestation and also educates the young in environment matters. VSD's priority in recent years has been the afforestation of several rural areas which directly results in the lessening of pollution. Their aim is to promote the 'one child one tree' philosophy by planting trees in open plains, empty land and around temples and schools prior to the onset of the monsoons. On average, 15–30,000 saplings are distributed annually, many of which are fruit-bearing trees, which in the longer term will benefit the local economy.

VSD have organised several speaking and essay competitions for children on subjects like 'planting trees', 'wealth of forests' and 'trees and creepers are our relatives'. Today, there are 125 VSD branches and a volunteer force of about 12,000.

Judaism

USA: The Development of the Environmental Sabbath

This is an initiative of Jewish groups in the USA, led primarily by the World Jewish Congress and the Union of American-Hebrew Congregations, in collaboration with the United Nations Environment Programme. It aims to encourage synagogues and temples, Jewish schools and other Jewish organisations to make one Sabbath each year the focus of environmental education, fundraising and action.

To promote this aim, an annual environmental Sabbath pack has been produced for the past nine years, which is distributed to over 6500 Jewish organisations.

At the suggestion of the World Jewish Congress, Jewish groups have been encouraged to hold their environmental Sabbath on *Rosh Hashanah*, which is traditionally observed as the celebration of the birthday of the world. Many synagogues and temples use the environmental Sabbath as the focus for up to three months of study, reflection and action on the environment.

Sikhism

India: Sikh University, New Town, Punjab

1999 sees the 300th anniversary of the foundation by Guru Gobind Singh of the Sikh Brotherhood known as the Khalsa. To commemorate this, the spiritual head of the Sikhs, Sri Singh Sahib Manjit Singh, the Jathedar, has launched a project to build a Sikh University dedicated to environmental studies in both the sciences and the humanities.

This university will form the heart of a new settlement, which itself will embody environmental principles such as solar power, energy from waste recycling and sustainable local building materials.

The settlement is planned for the beautiful area of Anandpur Sahib, in the Punjab, India. The site has already been purchased and an international team of environmental specialists are currently advising the Sikh community on some of the practical details, while the community itself works to develop an overall Sikh understanding of the demands of such an ambitious project.

Taoism

China: Sacred Mountains Project

For many thousands of years, certain major mountain ranges in China have been viewed as sacred. Traditionally, these have become known as the five Daoist sacred mountains and the four Buddhist. These mountain ranges also have immense ecological significance as natural habitats, forests and watersheds.

This project arose from the desire of the China Daoist Association to develop a coherent policy for the mountain ranges, which would combine respect for the natural and sacred significance of the sites with the needs of increasing numbers of visitors.

The project involves a major environmental and religious survey of seven of the sacred mountains and aims to inform the local authorities about the state of the mountains and help them to preserve them. Through publications and a possible documentary film, international attention will be drawn to the mountains.

As certain sacred mountains are included in UNESCO's 'World Cultural Heritage Programme', a liaison with UNESCO will be undertaken to produce educational material on both the religious and the environmental significance of the mountains.

CONTACTS AND FURTHER INFORMATION

The following publications give more detailed information about issues of religion and ecology. They can all be obtained from ICOREC (International Consultancy on Religion, Education and Culture) at the address shown below.

Buddha-Nature, Venerable Sucitto Bhikkhu, 1989. Reflections on the Buddhist Attitude to the Environment.

Seeds of Truth, Ranchor Prime, 1989. Lessons of ecology and plant management from the ancient Vedas of India.

World Religions and Ecology, Cassell, 1992. In this, the most comprehensive set of books on the major religions and ecology, leading authorities in each faith examine the basic teachings, historical examples and contemporary rethinking of each faith with regards to caring for the environment.

Buddhism and Ecology, edited by M. Batchelor and K. Brown

Christianity and Ecology, edited by E. Breuilly and M. Palmer

Hinduism and Ecology, edited by Ranchor Prime

Islam and Ecology, edited by F. Khalid with J. O'Brien

Judaism and Ecology, edited by Aubrey Rose

Faith and Nature, edited by Palmer, Nash and Hattingh. Rider, 1987. A collection of scriptural readings, prayers and prose, declarations and statements, liturgical materials and stories and legends drawn from the world's major faiths on the theme of our relationship with the natural world.

Genesis or Nemesis – belief, meaning and ecology, by Martin Palmer. Dryad, 1988. The way we treat the physical world depends on what we believe, and we need to widen our view to appreciate the positive elements of all the major world religions. Martin Palmer shows how basic themes from religion – celebration, repentance and hope – can be related to the practical work of caring for, or with, nature.

Worlds of Difference, by Martin Palmer and Esther Bisset. Blackie and Son, expanded edition 1989. Children's book which looks at how nine belief systems understand their relationship with the natural world. Accompanying Teachers' Guide.

Worlds of Choice, by Joannne O'Brien. Collins Educational, 1990. Outlines the hazards facing the living world and then focuses on the environmental practices and beliefs of nine communities worldwide whose future has been put at risk.

A Wealth of Faiths, J. O'Brien, M. Palmer, R. Prime. WF UK, 1992. What have the world's major faiths, the environment and economics got to do with each other? The answer is that without the guidance of the major religions, we could continue to live a lifestyle which will literally cost us the earth. For secondary schools.

After the Ark: Religious Understandings of Ourselves and Other Animals, Martin Palmer and Elizabeth Breuilly, Forbes Publications, 1996. Intended for Religious Education for 12–15 year olds; focuses on humanity's relationship with animals, seen from a multifaith perspective. Commissioned by and written in collaboration with Compassion in World Farming Trust.

To obtain any of these publications or for more information on the the Sacred Land project, contact:

> ICOREC
> Manchester Metropolitan University
> 799 Wilmslow Road
> Manchester M20 2RR
> United Kingdom
> TEL: 0161 434 0828
> FAX: 0161 434 8374

For details of WWF-UK's wide range of religious and educational publications:

> WWF
> Panda House
> Weyside Park
> Godalming
> Surrey GU7 1XR
> United Kingdom
> TEL: 01483 426444
> FAX: 01483 861006

For further details about the Holy Island project:

> Samye Ling Tibetan Centre
> Eskdalemuir
> Langholm
> Dumfrieshire DG13 0QL
> United Kingdom
> TEL: 013873 73232
> FAX: 013873 73223

For more information on Sacred Land and churchyard schemes:

> Church and Conservation Project
> Arthur Rank Centre
> National Agriculture Centre
> Stoneleigh Park
> Warwickshire CV8 2LZ
> United Kingdom
> TEL: 01203 696969

THE GROUND OF LOVE

For Rajwant, Balvinder and friends, singing

'The way is very muddy but I am in love with you,
What should I do?'* Here, in a back courtyard in Windsor,
In the falling grey light, between bursts of aeroplane,
You sing the Beloved song that has no end –
Your voices as quiet as the rain they transcend
Or as it falls in the softness of your faces and voices,
Where Love can spread a cloth out anywhere, on any ground.

* quotation from the *Guru Granth Sahib*

Jay Ramsay

TELL THE PEOPLE

Song lyric after Sam Younger, BBC World Service

Tell the people the day is dawning
Tell the people there isn't much time –

Tell the people the earth is beautiful
Tell them the rights of every child;

Tell the people we can go no further
Tell them we've gone out of our souls…

Tell the people that our world is breaking
Tell them we must find the way home

Tell the people 'we must love one another'
Tell them that there's no other way

Tell them the meaning of our story
Tell them before the Dawning Day

Tell them that the earth is our body
In every blade and tangle of grass;

Tell them what is outside is in us
And we're all going to share in it at last –

And if you tell them this, tell them gently,
Tell them so they don't run away:

Tell them that we are the Kingdom
And the Kingdom has come to stay.

Jay Ramsay

Epilogue

THE SIGN
with Xavier*

And then: after the end, after all we've said
If we can see it, and if we can't say it, utter it, speak it
It comes
             scored in two huge vapour trails across the blue –

Beyond the skein of our eyes as I call to you, look!
And the whole sky goes vertical
                              the two lines

Intersecting in a cross, with one trail bent
The other fading, but unmistakable
                              as we raise our heads

Together, a hundred yards apart, seeing it:

A cross for every faith in the blue of the higher mind,
A sign that You never forget us, however we forget.

* Walking to the library

Jay Ramsay

Declaration on Religion, Land and Conservation

The Conference on Religions, Land and Conservation
Ohito, Japan

Presented to the first Session of the Summit on Religions and Conservation
6th April, 1995

We the delegates to the Conference on Religions, Land and Conservation who have been meeting in Ohito, Japan since 28th March 1995, present this statement to you, the delegates of the first Session of the Summit on Religions and Conservation.

Our discussions were based on the spirit of co-responsibility discovered at Assisi in 1986. We are pleased to report that after having reiterated and discussed our respective faith traditions, we have achieved a consensus of principles and objectives common to our respective faiths. We offer this to the world community of faiths as a starting point for generating their own programmes of action.

We urge delegates to the Summit to adopt this statement and commend it to the Second Session in Windsor and draw it to the attention of representatives of both the religious and secular communities internationally.

Expressions of Concern
In particular, the health of the planet is being undermined by systemic breakdowns on several levels:

faith communities are not taking effective action to affirm the bond between humankind and nature, and lack accountability in this regard;

human systems continue to deteriorate, as evidenced by militarism, warfare, terrorism, refugee movement, violations of human rights, poverty, debt and continued domination by vested financial, economic and political interests;

biological systems and resources are being eroded, as evidenced by the ongoing depletion, fragmentation and pollution of natural systems.

Recognising the important parallels between cultural and biological diversity, we feel a special urgency with regard to the ongoing erosion of cultures and faith communities and their environmental traditions, including the knowledge of people living close to the land.

Spiritual Principles
(Not listed in order of priority)

As people of faith, we are called on to respond to these concerns. We recognize that humanity as a whole must face these concerns together. Therefore we recommend these principles as a basis for appropriate environmental policy, legislation and programmes, understanding that they may be expressed differently in each faith community.

1 Religious beliefs and traditions call us to care for the earth.

2 For people of faith maintaining and sustaining environmental life systems is a religious responsibility.

3 Nature should be treated with respect and compassion, thus forming a basis for our sense of responsibility for conserving plants, animals, land, water, air and energy.

4 Environmental understanding is enhanced when people learn from the example of prophets and of nature itself.

5 Markets and trade arrangements should reflect the spiritual needs of people and their communities to ensure health, justice and harmony. Justice and equity principles of faith traditions should be used for maintaining and sustaining environmental life systems.

6 People of faith should give more emphasis to a higher quality of life in preference to a higher standard of living, recognising that greed and avarice are root causes of environmental degradation and human debasement.

7 All faiths should fully recognise and promote the role of women in environmental sustainability.

8 People of faith should be involved in the conservation and development process. Development of the environment must take better account of its effects upon the community and its religious beliefs.

9 Faith communities should endorse multi-lateral consultation in a form that recognises the value of local/indigenous wisdom *and* current scientific information.

10 In the context of faith perspectives, emphasis should be given not only to the globalisation of human endeavours, but also to participatory community action.

Recommended Courses of Action

1 We call upon religious leaders to emphasise environmental issues within religious teaching: faith should be taught and practised as if nature mattered.

2 We call upon faith communities to commit themselves to sustainable practices and encourage community use of their land.

3 We call upon religious leaders to recognise the need for ongoing environmental education and training for themselves and all those engaged in religious instruction.

4 We call upon religious leaders and people of faith to promote environmental education within their community especially among their youth and children.

5 We call upon people of faith to implement individual, community and institutional action plans at local, national, and global levels that flow from their spiritual practices and where possible to work with other faith communities.

6 We call upon religious leaders and faith communities to pursue peacemaking as an essential component of conservation action;

7 We call upon religious leaders and communities to be actively involved in caring for the environment to sponsor sustainable food production and consumption.

8 We call upon people of faith to take up the challenge of instituting fair trading practices devoid of financial, economic and political exploitation.

9 We call upon the world's religious leaders and world institutions to establish and maintain a networking system that will encourage sustainable agriculture and environmental life systems.

10 We call upon faith communities to act immediately, to undertake self-review and auditing processes on conservation issues on a regular basis.

As we have found the first Conference on Religions, the Land and Conservation mutually beneficial, we recommend that this gathering be reconvened every five years. This meeting will serve as a review and auditing process to chart the progress of the faith communities and their religious leaders.

We commit ourselves individually and jointly to take the principles agreed upon at this gathering to our various situations and work towards implementing them.

We would encourage and welcome any projects and programmes which embody these principles and recommended courses of action.

CO-CHAIRMEN
Fazlun Khalid
Shoji Mizuno

BAHÁ'ÍS
Paul Hanley
Jimmy Seow

BUDDHISTS
Venerable Lobsang Gawa
Stephanie Kaza

CHRISTIANS
Lucian Gavrila
Eddie Idle
Pat Lupo, OSB

HINDUS
Shiba Sankar Chakraborty
Swami Akhandanand Savaswati Vankhandi Maharaj
Sanjay Rattan
Shri Sewak Sharan

JEWS
Meir Lipshatz

MUSLIMS
Abdur Razzaq Lubis
Fuad Nahdi
Mohammad Sharif Weideman

MOA
Shigenobu Kanayama
Teruo Taniguchi

CONFERENCE SECRETARY
Jo Edwards